The Powerful Book of

Hoodoo Spells

A Witch's Guide to Conjuring, Protection, Cleansing,
Justice, Love, and Success—Using Rootwork, Herbs,
Candles, Oils, and More

Layla Moon

Table of Contents

Chapter 9: Spells for Justice 156

Conclusion 163

Thank You 165

References 167

4 FREE Gifts

To help you along your spiritual journey, I've created 4 FREE bonus eBooks.

You can get instant access by signing up to my email newsletter below.

On top of the 4 free books, you will also receive weekly tips along with free book giveaways, discounts, and so much more.

All of these bonuses are 100% free with no strings attached. You don't need to provide any personal information except your email address.

To get your bonus, go to:

https://dreamlifepress.com/four-free-gifts

Or scan the QR code below

SCAN ME

Spirit Guides for Beginners: How to Hear the Universe's Call and Communicate with Your Spirit Guide and Guardian Angels

Guided by Moon herself, inspired by her own experiences and knowledge that has been passed down by hundreds of generations for thousands of years, you'll discover everything you need to know to;

- Understanding what the call of the universe is
- How to hear and comprehend it
- Knowing who and what your spirit guides and guardian angels are
- Learning how to connect, start a conversation, and listen to your guides
- How to manifest your dreams with the help of the cosmic source
- Learning how to start living the life you want to live
- And so much more…

Law of Attraction: Manifest Your Desire

Learn how to tap into the infinite power of the universe and manifest everything you want in life.

Includes:

- Law of Attraction: Manifest Your Desire ebook
- Law of Attraction Workbook
- Cheat sheets and checklists so make sure you're on the right path

Hoodoo Book of Spells for Beginners: Easy and effective Rootwork, Conjuring, and Protection Spells for Healing and Prosperity

Harness the power of one of the greatest magics. Hoodoo is a powerful force ideal for holding negativity at bay, promoting positivity in all areas in your life, offering protection to the things you love, and ultimately taking control of your destiny.

Inside, you will discover:

- How to get started with Hoodoo in your day-to-day life
- How to use conjuration spells to manifest the life you want to live
- How casting protection spells can help you withstand the toughest of times
- Break cycles of bad luck and promote good fortune throughout your life
- Hoodoo to encourage prosperity and financial stability
- How to heal using Hoodoo magic, both short-term and long-term traumas and troubles
- Remove curses and banish pain, suffering, and negativity from your life
- And so much more…

Book of Shadows

A printable PDF to support you in your spiritual transformation.

Within the pages, you will find:

- Potion and tinctures tracking sheet
- Essential oils log pages
- Herbs log pages
- Magical rituals and spiritual body goals checklist
- Tarot reading spread sheets
- Weekly moon and planetary cycle tracker
- And so much more

Get all the resources for FREE by visiting the link below

https://dreamlifepress.com/four-free-gifts

Beginning the Journey

Life is all about the journey, and mine has been one of adventure. It didn't start in the best of circumstances. I didn't grow up with much. Poverty is what most folks would call it today. We just called it surviving. I remember my mother struggling to provide for me and my siblings, working three jobs to make sure that there was food on the table. I remember wanting to spend more time with her.

However, my mother had her own demons to contend with. Aside from her multiple jobs, our extended family was not what you'd call a happy bunch. Dysfunction and toxic relationships abounded. My mother was no exception to the rule, and I watched as she went from one toxic man to the next, never finding what she was looking for. Even at a young age, I remember looking at the life I was dropped into and thinking, "I want more for myself."

It wasn't until many missed opportunities and bad decisions later that I finally found a path for myself that ensured a better future. I was in my mid-20s when I began my Hoodoo journey. It was after a particularly nasty breakup, stemming from one of those toxic relationships — the kind that only last as long as they do because you're complementing shades of dysfunction. I remember sitting at my kitchen table one night, in my shoebox apartment, thinking once again, "I want more for myself."

To better understand where I was, I decided to explore my family history. How did I come to be? It was suddenly a pressing question that I needed an answer to. I knew my mother hailed from Queens but beyond that, I knew very little about my family, aside from the few who would come to cause chaos in our world when I was a child.

What I discovered completely changed my direction in life, sending me on a path of victory and fulfillment. I had no idea what I was beginning that night I first started looking into my family. I had no idea that it would bring me to Hoodoo and the powerful effects I would see in my life as a result.

With the spiritualist practices of Hoodoo and the law of attraction, I began to see myself improve as a person. The desires that I manifested came to me, and I was on my way out of that shoebox apartment and onto better things. I began seeing opportunities everywhere and I took them. I crawled from the bottom to the life that I had envisioned as a little girl. A better life.

I want to take you on that same journey by sharing what I've learned throughout my own Hoodoo practice. These lessons that I share with you are invaluable. They will direct you down the path that you never dared walk before. I promise it isn't like what you see in the movies. Hoodoo magic is all about intention, proper preparation, and spirituality.

CHAPTER 1

Getting Started With Hoodoo

Hoodoo is the result of generations upon generations of practitioners building on the foundation of those who came before. It is so rich and broad that it can be daunting for those who are looking to start practicing, especially those who weren't exposed to it growing up. However, Hoodoo is a journey, not a destination. Throughout your life, as you practice, you'll learn and discover more about Hoodoo as a magical practice, a culture, a piece of black history, and a community.

Starting Hoodoo practice blind or without proper knowledge and respect of the practice can be dangerous. While, in recent years, Hoodoo has moved more into the mainstream as experienced practitioners work to preserve and celebrate this piece of black history, Hoodoo is still widely misunderstood. For one, Hoodoo is already plagued with misinformation rooted in racism and ignorance. This lack of understanding can cause real harm to Hoodoo practitioners and black culture as a whole. In addition to the social risk, Hoodoo also utilizes very real spiritual elements. If you play with powers that you don't understand, you risk harming yourself and the people around you. However, this isn't a reason to fear Hoodoo. With proper education and an open, curious mind, you can make your world a better place and take control of your life.

In this chapter, you'll learn everything you need to know about what Hoodoo is, how it's practiced, and how you can start practicing on your own. Consider this the first step on your journey.

What Is Hoodoo?

Hoodoo is a folk magic practice. Folk magic refers to a practice passed down from generation to generation, usually within a particular racial or ethnic group, that uses physical properties to affect the spiritual world. Most folk magic practices exist to remedy everyday problems, such as relationship strife and sickness. Though the terms are often mixed up, Hoodoo is distinct from Voodoo. Voodoo is a West African religion with its own religious systems, leaders, and pantheon. While Hoodoo does share some similarities to the core beliefs and philosophies of Voodoo due to its West African roots, Hoodoo is not a religion. Hoodoo practitioners can ascribe to any religious beliefs.

One of the most unique traits of Hoodoo is that it draws influences from many other cultures, from West Africa to Christianity, to Native American folk magic. This is because Hoodoo developed along with black culture. Hoodoo is a uniquely Western black practice. As black people were transported from West Africa to the Americas and fought for their survival, not only physically but spiritually, we shaped and were shaped by the other cultures we encountered. An exploration of the roots of Hoodoo is an exploration of black history.

African Roots

Much of the African elements of Hoodoo come from Central and Western Africa, where many black people were first kidnapped from their homeland and taken into chattel slavery.

For example, the beliefs of the Yoruba people continue to be reflected in modern Hoodoo practice. From them, we get the importance of crossroads. The Yoruba people give offerings to the trickster God, Eshu-Elegba, at crossroads as they believe that is where he resides, and many Hoodoo spells and rituals are supposed to be performed at crossroads. From the Igbo people, we get the practice of pouring libations over the graves of the dead, something that transcends Hoodoo and encompasses black culture as a whole.

From the Bantu-Kongo people, who made up an estimated 40% of all African enslaved people, we get the Kongo cosmogram. This symbol represents the rising and setting sun and the bounds between the physical and spiritual world, a visual representation of the various cosmic energies at work. Those symbols have been found in many historical black churches and plantations across the south.

Slavery and Christianity

While there are West African spiritual practices that survived in a similar form, much of Hoodoo is the result of the oppression of the black spirit. Slave owners and the dominant culture were invested in converting slaves to Christianity. The practice of native religions and even the speaking of native languages could risk serious punishment or even death. This pushed any spiritual practice that didn't strictly conform to Christianity underground. Native spirituality was practiced in the woods, under the cover of night, and never discussed in open spaces, lending an air of mystery that somewhat persists to this day. Another way that enslaved people managed to hold onto their native practices was by using Christianity to obscure them and combining the beliefs and practices of both.

Many Hoodoo practitioners are Christian, or at least utilize Hoodoo's Christian roots in their practice. The Bible is considered an important spiritual object, working as a talisman of protection as well as a spell book. Specifically, the Psalms are often used in spells and rituals. The biblical figure of Moses, the man who freed the slaves from Egypt, is important throughout black culture, but specifically in Hoodoo Christianity. Christian Hoodoo practitioners consider Moses as the best Hoodoo conjurer of all time as he performed magic and miracles.

Those who were brought to areas where Catholicism was the dominant form of Christianity had a unique experience when trying to hold onto their native practices. While the enforcement of the religion was somewhat restricted, the existence of the saints offered a unique way to preserve their worship of the Loa. Voodoo deities were ascribed to specific saints so that enslaved people could continue to worship them as they pleased.

Hoodoo was birthed out of a need to protect and care for our community when no one else would. While Hoodoo is a solitary practice and practitioners rarely work with others, they do work *for* others, healing those in need, punishing those who harm us, and offering protection through trials and tribulations.

Core Beliefs

While Hoodoo practitioners can ascribe to any religion, there are a few core beliefs that form the philosophical aspects of Hoodoo. These beliefs drive every ritual and spell and should inform every step you take in your practice.

Gods and Deities

The beliefs of Voodoo had the greatest impact on the evolution of modern Hoodoo. Many people misunderstand Voodoo as a polytheistic religion because of its many named deities. In reality, Voodoo sees God in all things. Our creator wants to be close to us, so he splits himself into several other beings to do so. These manifestations of God are called the Loa, and communicating with them is part of how we derive magical power.

Ancestors

Blood is the most powerful magical element. Our blood holds the story of who we are and where we came from as it connects us to our ancestors. It's incredibly difficult for many black people to trace their background. Detailed records were rarely kept for enslaved people and many of them have been lost to time and that lack of knowledge leaves us lost in our own lives. Hoodoo offers us a means of overcoming that barrier and finding ourselves.

Our ancestors are active and present in our lives and by connecting with them, we can tap into our true abilities. Our ancestors can offer us wisdom and guidance as they see things we do not. They can assist and reveal. However, to earn this goodwill and co-operation with them, they have to be treated with respect. In that way, they are like deities in their own right.

The importance of ancestors is a big part of why Hoodoo is a closed practice, meaning that it can only be practiced by those who descended from African slaves. Hoodoo does share a lot in common with other folk magic practices and those outside of the African diaspora can learn a lot about magic and black history through studying Hoodoo. However, because Hoodoo was born out of the unique experiences and suffering of black folks, it can only be passed down by them. Those who don't belong to this bloodline do not have access to the true spiritual power of Hoodoo; although by exploring their own lineage, they can find a practice that is their true birthright.

Intent

Your goals and intentions are incredibly powerful in Hoodoo. A spell that is created with the intent to only affect one person will only affect that person because of the power of your intent. Many spells call for you to express your intent. This can be through meditation, repeating a phrase or psalm, or writing it down. However, the spirits know your heart. If, deep down, your intent is different than what you claim, this can affect the outcome of your spell. It is important to understand what you want and to have clear, confident, and honest goals.

Vengeful Justice

Spells must also abide by the intent of God. Anything done with magic reflects the will of God. We see this in curses; Hoodoo allows practitioners to harm those who deserve it as a form of retribution. The punishment has to fit the crime to count as justice. Spells that harm people regardless of their ethics are referred to as "black magic." Black magic is dangerous and should be attempted by only the most experienced Hoodoo practitioners.

Divination

Hoodoo practitioners can communicate with spiritual beings, such as deities and ancestors, to learn things they cannot perceive in the physical world. This gives us knowledge of how they can manipulate the powers that be to reach their desired goals.

The Divine Providence

Regardless of what religion you ascribe to, Hoodoo relies on the existence of a supreme creator deity. This deity or deities have a vested interest in the lives and goings-on of human beings and are involved in every element of our lives.

Principle of Signatures

Our creator made everything in existence with its own mark or signature. This signature identifies the purpose and uses of everything. This is particularly important in rootwork or using plants and herbs in Hoodoo conjuring. Through your growth as a Hoodoo practitioner, you'll learn how to identify that signature in the natural world around you.

Afterlife

Our souls persist after our physical bodies die and enter a spiritual realm. While this realm is distinct from the physical one, we can still interact and communicate with the souls of those who have passed on.

Dispelling the Myths

Hoodoo is representative of the unbreakable spirit of black folks, and our ability to hold onto our culture and our power — regardless of our circumstances. This incredible power is a threat to a culture that seeks to hold us down and keep us from thriving and growing as a people. For this reason, our spiritual practices have been demonized throughout history.

From official laws banning the practice of native African religions to modern taboos, Hoodoo has developed a bad reputation. Hoodoo and Voodoo have become bad words, used to describe vague boogeymen in the media. Many people know nothing about Hoodoo except for what they see in mainstream media depictions, and this drives the belief that Hoodoo is dangerous, primitive, evil, or carnal. However, very little of what you see in the movies is true.

Hoodoo practitioners come from all walks of life, and are common people. They are churchgoers and community members who live and love the communities they serve. Hoodoo has long since been a form of healing and spiritual support in the black community. Much of the pop culture aesthetic of Hoodoo comes from certain practices in New Orleans such as Voodoo, Woodoo, and Vodun, all unique religions with their own beliefs and rituals. While some of these include things like animal sacrifices and depictions of the dead, they aren't anything like the devil-worshiping aesthetic we see in most depictions of black folk magic, and are distinct from Hoodoo.

There are many misunderstood Hoodoo practices that we will shed light on throughout this book. One of the most common negative associations with Hoodoo is that of graveyards. It is often depicted as sinister satanic rituals, evoking images of grave robbing, and dangerous nighttime rituals. In reality, Hoodoo conjurers see graveyards as an incredibly powerful site due to its connection to our ancestors. Certain spells might call for the dirt from a graveyard or a Hoodoo practitioner might speak wisdom by communing with the spirits. However, these are niche and somewhat uncommon practices, usually only done by experienced practitioners and always conducted with deep respect for those who rest there.

To put it simply, the overwhelming majority of depictions of Hoodoo that don't come directly from active practitioners are mostly fabrications created to scare people away from embracing their cultural power and stigmatize those who do. The best way to combat the negative effects of these lies is to see the truth for yourself.

Tools of Hoodoo

Hoodoo doesn't require expensive tools or complicated kits. Hoodoo was birthed out of a people who had less than nothing. No matter your circumstance, you can become a conjurer in your own way. There are a few tools that you'll want to seek out for your practice. These are the building blocks of your personal practice. Though we will be giving some specific suggestions, the exact materials will vary for every spell. As we go into more detail about how to use these different tools, you might find yourself drawn one way or another. You may find yourself called to be a true rootworker, working mainly with nature, or you might resonate more with candle magic. Regardless, these tools are simply your instruments for accessing your own spiritual power.

Altar

The most important part of any Hoodoo practice is your altar. Your altar will be where you commune with your deities and ancestors to access your power and wisdom. You might be tempted to skip the altar and go straight to the fun stuff, but an altar is mandatory. Our deities and ancestors are our guides and attempting to engage in magic without their help can be fruitless or even dangerous. While your prayers can be heard anywhere, communication through your altar is always strongest.

An altar is incredibly personal, and will reflect your unique beliefs, goals, and family; so, remember to trust your intuition. Here is a guide to creating your own spiritual altar:

Location

Select a location for your altar that has low traffic. You'll ideally want to be alone and undisturbed at your altar. However, you don't want to put it in your bedroom. The traffic of different energies and spirits can disrupt your sleep and cause strange or distressing dreams.

If you can't find an entirely separate room for your altar, you can use a closet, section off an area with room dividers or curtains, or place your altar in a designated cabinet or cupboard. You'll also want to make sure your altar is in a place you enjoy being, somewhere that offers you peace, comfort, and serenity.

Table

The base of your altar should be made of a natural material, a theme we'll explore with most other tools. Wood is the most common choice, but you can also use glass or wicker. Many practitioners prefer a waist-high table as this allows you to kneel in prayer, a sign of respect to both your ancestors and your deities.

Now that you've selected the base of your altar, you'll need to cleanse it of negative energy. There are many different oils and water that can be used to cleanse an object. Florida Water and Koloria 1800 have both been used for generations as cleansing and holy waters by Hoodoo practitioners, and can be purchased from many folk magic stores. Rub the liquid on the table in a clockwise motion. Once dry, say a prayer over your table and communicate that this is a holy space.

Trinkets and Tools

Lay a cloth down on your table. Again, something made of natural fibers is preferred. You can use the patterns and colors to express your personality or goals. Many people use African prints to represent their respect for their lost ancestry.

Next, add a Bible. This isn't a necessity. However, even if you aren't strictly Christian or, like many Hoodoo practitioners, have a different cultural relationship to Christianity, the Psalms make for powerful spells and can help you focus on your goals and connect to your spiritual self. Also, as many of your ancestors were probably Christian, a Bible will help create a comfortable and inviting space for them. They'll respond to verses that they are familiar with. It will also offer you protection from negative spirits.

Place a white, seven-day candle on your altar. White is the color of purity, and the light of the candle will serve as a beacon to the spiritual world. While you'll burn lots of different candles in your practice, you'll want to keep a seven-day candle burning at all times, so make sure to keep many on hand.

Add a glass of water to your altar. Water has great significance in Hoodoo and its West African religious roots. We enter the physical world from the spiritual one through the water of the womb. It represents an entryway or portal and will help ease communication through the realms.

Lastly, and the most fun part, you'll want to add items that specifically connect you to the deities you're going to work with. For your ancestors, you can include photos, personal effects, and items you know they interacted with or cared about.

Whenever two things come into contact, they remain eternally linked in some way, so these items will help draw your ancestors. Add as many of these for as many ancestors as you can. For many black people, it's hard to get photos of ancestors past two or three generations. However, even if you don't have pictures, you can write down names. If you have legal and safe access, you can also include dirt from the graves of your ancestors on your altar to strengthen that connection as well.

As a Hoodoo practitioner, you can work with any deities from whatever religion you believe in. Whatever deities you're working with, place symbols or trinkets that connect to them. This can include photos, like pictures of the spirits, or symbols like crosses or charms. You can even place a burning candle next to these pictures or items to enhance the connection. You can also include other items that you find spiritually significant like crystals, tarot cards, or conjuring bones.

Using Your Altar

Your altar will also be where you cast most of your spells. Some people set up dedicated altars for individual spells. These altars will be broken down after the spell is completed and are usually made of ritual-specific signifiers. For example, a red cloth for a love ritual, or green candles, incense, and herbs related to wealth for a money spell. These altars should be cleansed and constructed the same way even if they are put together sparsely.

There are many ways to utilize your altar. You'll want to make praying at your altar a part of your daily or weekly routine even if you aren't casting a spell that day. This will maintain an open communication with your deities. You don't want to go to them only when you need something. Your deities and ancestors should be a welcomed part of your life. Whether you spend this time meditating, making art, or praying, make sure to spend time with the spirits lending you your power.

Inviting Your Ancestors

When you first build your altar, you'll need to bring your ancestors to you. Once your ancestors are invited, they'll return when you call upon them. You can invite your ancestors with a three-day ritual once your altar is fully constructed. If you feel you've lost your connection with your ancestors or if you want to strengthen your relationship with one person in particular, you can repeat this process.

On day one, sit at your altar and meditate on your ancestors. Picture their faces and, if you have memories of them, take the time to appreciate those memories. Say their names out loud. You want them to know that they are remembered and appreciated.

On day two, cook two meals and take them to your altar. Take this opportunity to share a meal with your ancestors. Take as much time as you need in meditation and prayer until you feel you've achieved the start of a connection. Leave the plate of food out until it starts to go bad.

On the third day, bring your offerings to your ancestors. Your offerings can be generally valuable things like flowers, food, liquors, or candies. You can also use things you know your ancestors enjoyed, such as a favorite dish or a favorite perfume. You can also offer your own gifts through singing and dancing. Your offerings are an expression of gratitude for all the things they sacrificed for the life you have today. After you have given them your offerings, ask your ancestors to be a part of your practice. Say out loud that you would like their help and guidance.

Conclusion

Now that you understand the basics of Hoodoo, it's time to get to the actual practice. There are infinite different ways to interact with the spirits and utilize your personal power. As you learn more about what Hoodoo can do for you and how you can do it, you'll gain a better sense of what your personal goals are.

CHAPTER 2

Rootwork and Herb Magic

At the core of our modern pharmaceutical and medicinal practices are the gifts Mother Nature has given to us. Before we could separate natural herbs into their core components and combine them into modern medicines, we used the herbs themselves to keep ourselves and our communities healthy. However, herbs have more to offer us than just healing our physical bodies. They can also help to heal, guide, and empower us spiritually.

Rootwork

'Rootwork' is another term for Hoodoo that reflects the importance of the Earth. Rootworkers often lean on herb magic more than other forms of practice.

There's somewhat of an overlap between rootwork and Appalachian and Native American folk magic for many reasons. For one, Hoodoo was influenced by Native American folk magic due to our proximity to Native Americans and the few poor white folks who had to rely on their deep connection to the Earth to survive when their wealthy counterparts had access to modern medicines.

Even if you don't intend to make herbal magic the core of your practice, understanding the different associations and uses of herbs is important. Certain spells require certain herbs. Herbal understanding will help you be purposeful about your use of incense or herbal oils. It will also give you a broader picture of the depth and breadth of Hoodoo.

Getting Your Herbs

The first step of herbal magic is getting your hands on the right herbs. Some people consider themselves kitchen witches, using common spices in their spells instead of freshly growing or picking them. While this is a perfectly valid form of practice, there are some drawbacks to this approach. For one, there are lots of spiritually powerful herbs that you simply can't buy at a grocery store. Cheaper store-bought herbs may also be made of low-quality plants, or mixed with fillers. Store bought herbs also don't have the added spiritual benefit of imbuing your intent into your herbs. If you're going to buy your herbs, make sure to consider if the herbs were collected and handled ethically, as the negative energies of unethical practices might get in the way of your practice.

When you grow your own herbs, your goals, intentions, and power will influence the herbs for their entire lifetime. This allows you to keep your favorite herbs on hand, making performing your most common spells easier. There is also power in picking herbs in the wild.

Wildcrafting

'Wildcrafting' or foraging refers to picking plants in the wild. This is a great way to get your herbs, as you know the plants you're getting are pure, organic, and not causing harm to the environment. They are the strongest they can possibly be because they are connected to the Earth as they should be. You also have the chance to get out into nature and recharge physically, mentally, and spiritually. Foraging for the right plants can be difficult depending on where you live, so it's important to educate yourself before you start going into the woods and picking things.

Research the flora that grows in your area. Make sure you know what plants bloom at what time of year and how you can differentiate similar plants. It can be very dangerous to pick wild herbs if you don't know enough about what plants look like in the wild and how to tell poisonous from benign plants. Keep a plant guide on you at all times and make sure to double-check. Consider bringing a more experienced forager with you the first couple of times to avoid making dangerous mistakes.

Wild animals also pose a threat in many areas. Even if there aren't many predators in the area, you still need some sort of self-defense, such as bells or bear spray. You should also make sure that you are allowed to be on whatever land you're foraging on. There could also be laws about picking certain plants that might be endangered or otherwise protected. Know your local laws and keep yourself out of trouble.

When you pick wild herbs, thank the Earth for its gifts. Say a prayer every time you pick something and never take more than you'll use. You can scatter seeds or give praise through singing or dancing to show your gratitude.

Drying Herbs

If you're working with fresh herbs, you'll need to store and care for them thoughtfully so that they don't spoil and lose their essence. You might be tempted to hoard as many herbs as you can and stockpile for the future. However, even preserved herbs have a limited shelf life and, if you're wildcrafting, you don't want to harm the environment. Drying and storing herbs will be a semi-regular practice in your journey.

The first step is picking your herbs when they're at peak ripeness. This will be different for every plant and will be affected by the climate so, it might be helpful to get a farmer's almanac. You want to harvest your herbs in the morning after the dew has evaporated but before they've been dried out by the sun. Use a knife or very sharp shears instead of ripping or tearing the plant to keep from damaging it. Don't cut more than ⅔ of the plant, or you risk killing it entirely. When growing your own herbs, you can cut off the flowers as they grow to ensure the herb produces more leaves than flowers.

With your herbs harvested, wash them with cool water and pat them dry with paper towels. Remove any leaves that might be damaged or sickly. These are usually on the bottom. Now it's time to dry them so that there is no excess moisture that could cause them to spoil.

Air Drying

Tie your herbs into bunches loosely enough that air can still move through them, and hang them up somewhere that is warm and dry, but away from direct sunlight; such as a well-ventilated attic or garage. You can put a paper bag with holes poked in it around the bundle to keep them from getting contaminated or dusty. This will also help you catch any seeds that may fall during the drying process. The setback with this approach is, while it will yield the most powerful herbs, it also takes the longest time. Certain herbs may take up to a month to completely dry out. You'll know they're completely dry when the stem breaks when bent and the leaves crumble when handled.

Tray Drying

This is a really good method for drying loose leaf herbs that can't be hung in bundles, but can also be used for stemmed herbs as well. Simply place them on a tray and hang them somewhere warm and dry. You might need to flip them throughout to make sure they're uniformly dry.

Oven Drying

You can also use added heat to dry your herbs. This does risk burning the herbs or releasing some of their natural oils, but it's much faster than air drying, and is useful in a pinch or if you don't have an appropriate area to dry your herbs. To use the oven, preheat to 90–110 degrees Fahrenheit. Any higher risks burning the herbs. If your oven doesn't go low enough, you can try leaving the oven door slightly open to keep the temperature low. Depending on the herbs, this will take 3–4 hours.

Microwave Drying

While this isn't an ideal manner of drying, this works well for getting small amounts of herbs dried quickly and is best used with loose leaves. You'll first want to make sure your herbs are completely dry on the outside after you wash them. Otherwise, your herbs will be cooked instead of dried. Put your herbs between paper towels and microwave on high for about 1–3 minutes depending on the thickness of the herb. Stop the microwave every 20–30 seconds to make sure they're not being overcooked.

Dehydrator

This is another great option for drying herbs. Make sure to read the specific instructions for your dehydrator to avoid mistakes. Place your herbs in a single layer without any overlap to make sure they dry evenly. If your herbs are very small or your dehydrator is built for larger items, you might need to place a screen into it to prevent the herbs from falling through the cracks. Herbs should be dried on the lowest setting, between 95 and 115 degrees Fahrenheit.

Drying Seeds

As we've said, you can use paper bags to catch seeds as they fall while drying your herbs. Once the herb is dried, give it a shake to drop all the seeds. Next, rub the seeds gently so you can take them out of their capsules. Lay them out on a paper towel and leave them in a warm, dry place until they're brittle and completely dry.

Storing Herbs

Now that your herbs have been prepared, you need to store them appropriately so that you have enough time to use them. Put your herbs into a dark-colored air-tight container, preferably a glass jar. You don't want your herbs to get too much direct sunlight as this will speed up the decaying process. Plastic containers can also risk contaminating your herbs with chemicals. Place them somewhere cool and use them as needed.

Common Herbs

There are way too many herbs with healing and spiritual properties that we cannot list them all. However, we'll go over some of the most common herbs, not only in Hoodoo, but in folk magic in general.

Ash

The Ash is a flowering tree related to olives and lilacs. It is associated with travel, protection, luck, as well as water and the ocean. The leaves, bark, and wood of these trees can be used in rituals to enhance their effect.

Adam and Eve Root

This is a type of orchid, most common in the Appalachian Mountains. It is also known as folk putty. This is a feminine plant associated with love and romance. Carrying the root can help you attract love. The flowers can also be used in love spells to address romantic strife.

Anise

Anise is a flowering plant that grows primarily in the Mediterranean and southwest Asia. It is commonly used as a flavoring, and tastes like licorice. Anise is associated with calm and comfort, and it stimulates spiritual awareness. You can put it in your pillow to help ward off bad dreams or burn it as incense to create a positive, happy environment.

Ague

Ague is a purple flowering plant that grows across North America. It is associated with protection and breaking curses.

Apple

Both the apple and its blossoms can be used in spell magic. It's associated with love, healing, sexuality, and fertility. It can also help stimulate your spiritual awareness to increase your powers of divination.

Angelica Root

Angelica, also called wild celery, is a sweet and edible plant that grows across Europe. It attracts luck and can help protect you. It is also a feminine herb that can help enhance your power as a woman.

Allspice

Allspice is a pepper plant that grows in many warm parts of the world and is used in lots of common spice mixes. You can use its pepper kernels, whole leaves, and branches. It's most strongly associated with luck and money, and is used in many spells and charms that seek to attract prosperity.

Aloe

Aloe is said to attract luck and prosperity, and can be added to a spell to increase the chances of getting your desired outcome and achieving success. Growing aloe vera in the home can help the inhabitants live luckier lives. It can also provide protection.

Alfalfa

Alfalfa sprouts are a common garnish, part of the legume family. They can be used to protect you from poverty and attract prosperity and wealth.

Almond

Almonds can assist in healing through the spiritual realm. They are also associated with wisdom, wealth, and prosperity.

Bay Leaf

Bay leaves are most strongly associated with wealth and are called upon in many money and prosperity spells. You can write your intentions on the leaf itself while doing a spell. They also provide protection and can enhance spiritual power.

Buckthorn

Buckthorn is a type of shrub with black or red berries that grows primarily in subtropical areas. It is heavily associated with luck and making wishes. It is also commonly used for spells seeking a good outcome in a court battle.

Bergamot

Bergamot is a citrus fruit that has commonly been used in food flavoring, perfumes, and cosmetics. While it's most commonly found in its essential oil form, you can also use the leaves in your spells. Bergamot can help improve your mental functions, promote good memory, and restful sleep. It is also associated with luck, success, and wealth.

Basil

Basil has been used to ease menstrual cramps for generations. It is also associated with love and romance, and can be used for divination to determine the state of a relationship. It can also help protect from negative energies and provide personal strength.

Bamboo

Bamboo grows easily and quickly. Keeping a bamboo plant in your home can help provide protection and health. This magical energy can be imbued into any tools built with bamboo such as magic staffs or furniture. You can also carve wishes into bamboo and incorporate this into your spells.

Buckeye

Buckeye is the name of both the tree and its nuts. Buckeye nuts are used in spells related to wealth and money, and are often carried around in the wallet as charms to attract prosperity.

Belladonna

Belladonna, also known as Deadly Nightshade, is a poisonous plant with purplish black berries and small purple flowers. While it is incredibly dangerous even in small doses, it is a very useful magical tool. It is associated with divination, psychic ability, and protection.

Balm of Gilead Tears

Balm of Gilead Tears (named so because of their teardrop shape) are the buds that grow from the Arabian balsam tree. It is often used in perfumes as well as magic. It is associated with protection as well as emotional and physical healing. The oil of Balm of Gilead can also be used as a consecrating or blessing oil to help attract spirits.

Balsam Fir

Balsam fir can be used as essential oils or full needles. It is associated with strength, insight, and bringing about personal change.

Comfrey

Comfrey is a very common and easy to grow medicinal plant used to help the body's natural healing abilities for flesh wounds as well as broken bones. This might be why it has long been associated with travelers. It can also help with restful, peaceful sleep, and is used in divination and prophetic spells.

Citronella

Citronella can be used as essential oils or whole leaves. They are associated with self-expression and mental clarity, making them very popular with artists. It can also cleanse your environment of negativity.

Calendula

Calendulas, also known as marigolds, are a type of yellow flower in the daisy family. They are used for protection and can be hung in doorways or windows to ward off negative spirits.

Camphor

Camphor trees are native to Asia but grow all around the world, particularly in the Southern United States. It's known for its thick, waxy green leaves and white flowers. Camphor is most commonly used as essential oils and incense. It can intensify your divination and connection with the spiritual world as well as act as a cleansing herb.

Cloves

Cloves are the dried flower buds from the Syzygium Aromaticum, an evergreen native to Indonesia. They are most commonly used as a culinary spice and perfume, though they have a white range of magic uses. They are used in protection spells and for cleansing of negative spirits. Spells meant to stop those who mean you harm often call for cloves.

Chili Pepper

Chili peppers are magically associated with love and romance, breaking curses, and providing protection against spiritual attacks.

Clover

Clovers have been used to heal both gastrointestinal problems and skin conditions. The three-leafed clover is seen as a symbol of the holy trinity. Along with attracting good luck, green clovers are associated with wealth, whereas red clovers can be used in spells related to love, sex, and romance.

Cayenne

Cayenne can speed up or intensify the results of a spell. It is associated with separation and repelling negativity. Cayenne is often used in spells meant to deflect or reverse spiritual attacks.

Cinnamon

Cinnamon is associated with passion, power, luck, and stimulation. You can use both powdered cinnamon or whole cinnamon sticks in your spells, depending on your needs. Cinnamon incense can help open your mind and bring passion into your spellcasting.

Chamomile

Chamomile is physically, mentally, and spiritually calming. Chamomile can be used to center your mind and get rid of anxiety and negative energy that might get in the way of your spell's success. It can also help attract positivity like love and friendship.

Coriander

Coriander is an herb similar to parsley. The ground leaves and seeds are most often used as a spice, but you can use the entire plant in your spells. Coriander is associated with peace and can help heal strife and conflict. It can also help attract a lover or heal a broken affair.

Catnip

Catnip, related to mint and spearmint, has been used medicinally to soothe stomach issues and colicky babies. It is also useful for those working with cat-related deities, like the Egyptian Goddess Bastet. Catnip is associated with protection, willpower, and luck.

Caraway

Caraway, also known as meridian fennel, has long, thin stalks and small white flowers. It is associated with wellness of the mind and can be used to improve sleep and remember dreams. It can also protect and be used to consecrate ritual tools.

Cypress

Cypresses are a type of Evergreen that grows across the Northern Hemisphere. Both the needles and the wood can be used in magic. It is often associated with death and mourning, and can help facilitate healing after a loss and connection with the departed.

Cumin

Cumin seeds can help prevent an object from being stolen and can be used in spells related to protection and warding off evil spirits. It can also be used in love potions.

Daisy

Daisies are associated with innocence and are often used in spells related to babies and children. They promote and attract love and can provide protection.

Daffodil

When hung around the home, daffodils can help attract luck, protect against negativity, and help with fertility.

Dogwood

Dogwoods are a woody species of evergreen with small white flowers and berry fruits, some of which are toxic. They grow throughout Eurasia and North America. You can use dogwood as incense, essential oil, wood, powdered bark, or dried flowers for spells related to protection and wishes.

Dill

Dill is associated with protection, wealth, and good luck. It can also be used to attract a lover and encourage lust and attractiveness.

Dragon's Blood

Dragon's blood, named after its bright red color, is a resin derived from the flowering Calamus plant. It is used most commonly as incense but can also work as pigment and medicine. You can find dragon's blood in oil, powdered resin, whole resin crystals, and incense forms. It is associated with energy and can be burned to increase your spiritual power during a spell, or to make magic ink. It also purifies and offers protection.

Eucalyptus

Eucalyptus is a type of flowering plant native to Australia and can be used as incense, essential oil, candles, or whole leaves. Eucalyptus is associated with healing, protection, and purification.

Echinacea

Echinacea, a type of daisy also known as coneflowers, is found throughout North America. Its bright pink petals are associated with attracting wealth and luck, and can be added to your spells and charms to strengthen them.

Fennel

You can use both the seed and the entire fennel plant in spells related to strength, vitality, and virility. It can also provide protection, ward off evil spirits, and help strengthen your own resolve and will.

Fern

Ferns are a popular house plant as they are hardy and relatively easy to grow. Ferns dispel negativity and can purify an area. They also promote mental clarity and focus.

Frankincense

Frankincense has an incredibly long history as a spiritually and magically significant substance. Similar to Dragon's Blood, it is a resin derived from the Boswellia tree and used in perfumes and incense. It can be used in the form of oil, whole resin, or crushed resin to cleanse, purify, and consecrate your spellcasting space. It has been used by traditional physicians to alienate anxiety and depression. It also attracts success and can aid in mediation, willpower, and self-control.

Gardenia

Gardenia is related to the coffee family and sports white or pale yellow flowers. It is associated with peace and can help protect you from strife and conflict as well as bring comfort in a difficult situation. It can also intensify healing spells.

Garlic

Garlic brings protection and healing. It is used in rituals meant to ward off the evil eye and negative spirits. It can also help facilitate healing and wellness.

Garden Sage

While the most commonly used type of sage is white sage, they are not the only ones that can be used for magical purposes. This is important to consider as white sage is specifically important to Native American communities and can currently be very difficult to access and cultivate. Sage is a popular smudging herb used to cleanse and purify an area. It is also associated with mental stability, wisdom, and healing, and can be used in times of strife or turmoil. You can also write on a sage leaf for a spell.

Galangal Root

Galangal root is in the ginger family, and has been used both in cuisine and medicine across Asia. It is heavily associated with justice and can be used to ensure success in a court case. It can also help stimulate your spiritual abilities, provide protection, and attract wealth.

Geranium

Also known as cranesbills, its flowers are either white, pink, blue, or purple, and grow in temperate and mountainous regions. They are associated with emotional and spiritual balance.

Ginseng

Ginseng is another ginger-like root. It is associated with masculinity, and is often used to increase male potency and virility, as well as attract lovers. It is also associated with wealth and healing.

Heather

This flowering shrub grows across Eurasia and has purple or white bell-shaped flowers. They are associated with protection, luck, and rain.

Hyacinth

Hyacinths are a spring-blooming flower that grow across the Mediterranean with clusters of blue, pink, or white petals. Hyacinths were named after Hiakintos, the Greek God of gay men. It can be used to attract love, luck, and success and help ease pain and grief.

High John the Conqueror Root

John is a black folklore hero. While stories differ, John is a trickster figure whose spirit was never broken by slavery. The plant itself is related to the sweet potato and has several uses in Hoodoo. It is said to bring good luck and prosperity, and is associated with masculinity.

Honeysuckle

Honeysuckles are associated with willpower, strength, and confidence. They can also be used in spells for money and success.

Hyssop

Hyssop grows pink, blue, or white flowers on a long, tall stalk. It has had many medical uses over time, including as an antiseptic and cough reliever. It is a cleansing herb and promotes spiritual openness. Hyssop can be used to bless or consecrate ritual items and help purge negative energy and spirits.

Iris

Irises are named after the Greek Goddess of rainbows. They are also purifying flowers and are associated with happiness, faith, and wisdom. They are often used in spells for infants.

Ivy

There are many types of ivy, many of which can be grown indoors to repel negative energies and provide protection as well as promote love, healing, and fertility, making them popular magical gifts for newlyweds.

Juniper

Junipers are aromatic evergreens. You can use both the needles and Juniper berry essential oils. Juniper attracts positive energy and prosperity, and helps protect against theft. Juniper berries are also associated with male potency.

Kava Kava

Kava kava is a root from the Pacific Islands, often brewed into a tea used for spiritual openness, socializing, and medicinal effects. It is used for spiritual enlightenment, and is associated with success and prosperity.

Lavender

Lavender is associated with peace and relaxation, and can be used to help calm anxieties that might get in the way of spellcasting. It is also associated with love, healing, and purification.

Lily of Valley

Lily of the valley, also known as lily of the field, has white, bell-shaped flowers and grows across the Northern Hemisphere, though it is invasive in North America. It is associated with peace and tranquility and can help soothe conflict and promote happiness.

Mugwort

Mugwort has been associated with the moon and femininity, due in part to it being used to treat female reproductive issues. Outside of its feminine and medical associations, mugwort is associated with divination, dreams, and harmony between the physical and spiritual world.

Mistletoe

Mistletoe is associated with creativity and fertility. It can be used to provide protection, particularly from illness, unwanted attention, or the evil eye. It can also be used to attract prosperity to a business.

Mustard Seed

Mustard seed is associated with strength, will, and bravery. It can be used to protect you against injury and encourages faithfulness, which will lead to success. Black mustard is also associated with confusion, and can be used to destabilize an enemy.

Myrrh

Myrrh is a resin made of sap from certain trees. It has been used medicinally for tooth care as well as heart and blood conditions. It is a sacred substance often used to create a space conducive to spiritual power. It enhances the power of other spells and rituals, and can be used to consecrate and bless ritual items.

Mandrake

Mandrakes are flower plants with yellow or orange berries. It is native to the Mediterranean and has been used medicinally to treat liver and gastrointestinal disorders. The root of the plant is usually used medicinally because this is where most of the medicinal compounds lie. For magic, it is because the mandrake root often resembles the human body. Mandrake can be used for protection and warding off evil. It is also associated with love and fertility.

Peppermint

Peppermint is used to purify and increase the spiritual energy of a place or a spell. It can also be used to promote peaceful sleep and prophetic dreams, as well as attract love and abundance.

Patchouli

Patchouli is commonly in the form of incense, essential oil, or resin and is known for its strong, woody smell. Patchouli can repel negativity and attract wealth and prosperity. It can also help with grounding and bringing one into better awareness of their physical world.

Parsley

Parsley is associated with physical and spiritual well-being. It can be used to increase vitality and strength, promote healing, and boost energy. It can also be used in lust or love spells to make you more attractive.

Rosemary

Rosemary is a purifying herb and is often used in smudging to cleanse an area before a ritual. It is associated with lust and romance and can be used in spells meant to attract a partner. It can also be used to bring mental clarity, prevent nightmares, and improve memory.

Rue

Rue is an ornamental and medicinal herb native to the Balkans. It is associated with protection, particularly against the evil eye, and can help banish negative spirits and bad habits. It can also enhance healing and break curses.

St. John's Wort

St. John's Wort is a yellow flowering plant that is used as supplements, oils, and whole. It is most commonly used medicinally as an antidepressant. It can be used for protection and warding off negative spirits as well as enhancing personal strength and bravery.

Sandalwood

Sandalwood can be used in the form of essential oils, sawdust, incense, or whole pieces of wood. It is associated with wishes, healing, and creating a healthy spiritual environment.

Tobacco

Tobacco is a protective herb and promotes strength and peace. It can also help establish communication with spirits and deities.

Thyme

Thyme is associated with love, friendship, and healthy relationships. It can be used to purify an area and attract good health. It can also promote restful sleep and offer protection from nightmares.

Tonka Bean

Tonka beans are commonly used in spices and perfumes. They are associated with love, courage, and prosperity. They are often used in spells to attract good fortune and luck.

Violets

Violets are related to peace, tranquility, and creativity. They can be used to inspire prophetic dreams and ward off nightmares. They can be used to purify a space, facilitating a proper headspace for spellcasting. It can also be used to bring good luck to newlyweds and infants.

Valerian

Valerians are sweet pink or white flowers, and the extract of the root is used medicinally for its calming and sedative effects. It is associated with dreams and harmony. They can be used in spells to settle arguments, calm strong emotions, and purify a space.

Wormwood

Wormwood grows in temperate conditions around the world and is used as a flavoring in many alcohols, including absinthe and vermouth, despite being somewhat toxic. It has also been used to treat infections and gastrointestinal issues. It is used to combat negativity, anger, violence, and the effects of the evil eye.

Yarrow

Yarrow grows with bundles of small white or pink flowers, and has been used medicinally and magically for generations. It's associated with courage, protection, and can ward off negative energy. It is also associated with love, making it a common gift for newlyweds. It is also used as an ingredient in spells for fidelity and peace in a relationship.

Using Herbs

Herbs are called upon in many more complicated spells, but you can also use herbs to utilize your spiritual power and take control over your life. Herb spells are relatively simple and can be incredibly powerful when performed with thoughtful intention. It may be tempting to combine a bunch of herbs into one spell or charm to get everything you want at once, but the conflicting energies can nullify the effects of a ritual/spell or result in negative results. If you are feeling confused or unsure about a spell you're casting, you can also call upon your ancestors for wisdom.

Here are some of the many simple ways you can use herbs to address the most common mental, physical, and spiritual needs.

Health and Wellness

- To ease anxiety or panic attacks, drink valerian tea.

- To help relieve stress and promote restful sleep, put sprigs of lavender under your pillow.

- Keep a jar of rosemary next to your bed to promote restful sleep.

- Brew comfrey tea to promote your body's natural healing abilities. You can also place the pressed juice onto small cuts.

- Rub goldenseal leaves on small cuts and abrasions to promote healing.

- Use heated eucalyptus oil or boil eucalyptus leaves to relieve congestion.

- Make a decoction by boiling parthenium down in water and sweetening it with honey or sugar. Use this mixture to soothe sore throats or coughs.

- Chew peppermint leaves to freshen and clean your teeth.

- Use mugwort in a ritual bath to deal with stressful dreams or nightmares.

Beauty

- Steep 2–3 tablespoons of fresh rosemary in a cup of boiling water for 10 minutes and add between ⅛ and ¼ cup of witch hazel to make an astringent to brighten the skin and calm irritation and eczema.

- Ginseng incense: burn the plant in a cauldron or utilize ginseng oil to make yourself more attractive to men.

- Mix a very fine sandalwood powder with rose or camphor oil and use it as a cleanser.

- Refresh your skin by rubbing catnip on your face.

Divination and Spiritual Wisdom

- When trying to communicate with the spirits, burn sage to intensify your spiritual connections.

- Place mugwort under your pillow to inspire prophetic dreams.

- If you're struggling to make a major decision, place jasmine in your pillow to achieve clarity.

- Heliotrope can be used to reach out to deities and seek prophetic wisdom.

Luck

- To attract good luck to your household, hang a branch of hazel above your door. You can also carry a hazelnut for the same effect.

- Make food and drinks with pomegranate seeds to attract prosperity.

- Hang holly branches throughout your home to attract good luck.

- Place sprigs of snakeroot, also known as black cohosh, around your home to ward off bad luck and negativity.

- To ensure success when gambling or playing a game, wash your hands with chamomile tea before you play.

- Carry clovers in your wallet to attract good luck wherever you go.

- Place a whole nutmeg in your pocket or put nutmeg powder in your shoe before you gamble to ensure success.

- To attract good luck to your home, grow sunflowers around your property. Pick them at sunset and wear them the next day to carry that good luck with you.

- Carry a buckeye to better your chances of winning when gambling.

Money

- Rub your money with a bergamot leaf to make sure it comes back to you. You can also leave the leaf in your wallet to attract money.

- Carry seven allspice kernels in your pocket or tied in your shirt for seven days. After the seven days, throw the kernels into running water and make a wish on how you'd like your money to manifest.

- Make a mixture of cinnamon and sugar. Sprinkle it on your money and shake it in the doorway of your home or business to attract prosperity.

- Burn laurel leaf or bay leaf in the form of incense or in

a cauldron while doing money spells to increase the likelihood of success.

- Grow alfalfa in and around your home to make sure you always have money.

- Make diluted tea with Thyme leaves and add it into the water when you wash your work clothes to attract financial success.

- Brew chamomile tea and sprinkle it around your home to attract money into your household.

- Sprinkle crushed basil around your home to attract money to your household.

- Place clovers in your wallet or grow them around your property to attract prosperity.

Love

- Make an apple blossom tea, burn apple blossom incense, or burn it in a cauldron to strengthen a love spell.

- Carry lavender with you to attract love.

- To ensure the object of your affection takes interest in you, carry tulips near your skin when you interact with them.

- Plant bleeding heart flowers near your front door to attract love into your home.

- Wear violets, daisies, and daffodils in your hair to attract the attention of a new lover.

- Place vanilla oil behind your ears to enhance your attractiveness.

- Take a bath with a few dill seeds to enhance your magical abilities related to love.

- Make a cake with cinnamon, allspice, and cloves and give it to the object of your desire to attract their attention.

- Use Yarrow in your rituals to call upon deities related to love such as Venus or Aphrodite.

- Take Yohimbe bark in the form of a powder or tincture to enhance male potency.

- To prepare a damaged relationship, burn sweet annie (sweet wormwood) in your cauldron while saying a prayer for the relationship to heal.

- Make a potpourri of citrus peels to attract and strengthen friendships.

Protection and Strength

- Keep mandrake plants around your home or place one under your doormat to protect your household.

- Keep an aloe plant in your home to protect everyone inside from common accidents.

- To ward off negativity or spiritual attacks, place mugwort under your pillow.

- Carry or burn thistle to enhance your mental and spiritual strength.

- Hang an onion braid in your home to protect its inhabitants.

- An oak tree on your property will help strengthen you and those you live with. You can also carry an acorn with you for strength.

- Carry a bay leaf in your pocket to enhance your confidence.

- Place some cinnamon sticks under your bed to enhance your daily confidence.

- Plant hyssop around your house to protect it. Carry the hyssop in your pocket to take that protection with you.

- If you feel you're under spiritual or magical attack, place heather in your pillow.

Justice

- In a court case, carry High John the Conqueror Root to increase your chances of success.

- Chew some ginger and spit it out on the courtroom floor (discreetly) to ensure the fairest outcome.

- Bathe in chamomile before a court appearance to ensure a positive outcome.

Success

- To boost your success at work, put a few Hawthorn sprigs under your desk.

- For an extra advantage in your professional goals, write or carve what you hope to achieve on a piece of sandalwood. Place the sandalwood into a cauldron on your altar or a brazier and burn it. As the smoke goes up, your goals will be carried up to be heard by the spirits.

- Write the job or promotion you want onto a bay leaf and carry it around in your pocket.

- Place a sprig of peppermint above the door of your business or plant peppermint in and around the property to attract business.

- To succeed in a job interview, keep a pecan in your pocket.

- Keep a basil plant near your workspace to help you overcome challenges in your work.

- To ensure your best possible performance at work, in a meeting, or in an interview, carry a few pieces of frankincense resin.

Herb Garlands

An Herb Garland is a great way to use magic to benefit your home and surround yourself with spiritual power. You can make a ritual out of creating your herb garland by cleansing the area and focusing on your intentions while you put the garland together. To make an herb garland, you'll need to use whole bundles of, preferably fresh, herbs. Tie the bundles together with ribbon and tie them to a wreath frame with floral wire. Generally, you shouldn't use more than 3 or 4 different herbs in the same bundle as you don't want conflicting energies to get in the way of achieving your desire. Here are your options depending on what you want to do for your household.

- **For Healing Use**: Eucalyptus, Allspice, Rosemary, Rue, Lady's Mantles, Sandalwood, Peppermint, Wintergreen, Goldenseal, Comfrey, Lavender, Barley,

Apple Blossoms.

- **For Protection Use**: Onion, Mugwort, Betony, Valerian, Aloe Vera, Sandalwood, Snapdragon, Fleabane, Hyssop, Mandrake, Garlic, Cornflower, Mistletoe, Dill.

- **For Love Use**: Bleeding Heart, Peppermint, Tulip, Violet Catnip Yarrow, Lavender, Daffodil, Fig, Valerian, Basil, Clove, Periwinkle, Apple Blossom, Tulip.

- **For Prosperity Use**: Myrtle, Apple, Mint, Chamomile, Basil, Clover, Tonka Bean, Laurel Leaf/ Bay Leaf, Buckeye, Sunflower.

Conclusion

There's a reason our Hoodoo journey starts with rootwork. Herbs are some of the most powerful gifts the Earth has given us to allow us to take control of our lives physically, mentally, and spiritually. A good understanding of rootwork and the different uses of each herb will be an invaluable skill as a Hoodoo practitioner. The meaning of herbs will help inform your use of incense and oils. They are also called upon for many different spells and rituals, as we will discover.

CHAPTER 3

Conjure Oils and Oil Magic

Across time, in almost all religions, we see the sacredness of oils. Oil anointing is seen throughout the bible and is practiced to this day to offer blessings and purifications. There was a time when oils were only used by the highest priests and holy leaders, but now the power of holy oils has become available to people of all backgrounds. In modern times, oils are mostly used for aromatherapy. Most people understand how aromatic oils can influence your emotions and even treat mild medical ailments. However, the spiritual importance of oil is less known.

Basics of Oil Magic

There are many terms for magically significant oils, including conjuring oils, anointing oils, and conditioning oils (oils that are meant to deal with specific conditions). Oils represent a meeting of the spiritual and the physical. They are made by extracting the essence of a plant and diluting it with a base oil to transfer the properties of those herbs.

In Hoodoo, oils are a type of sealing. By applying oils onto something, we seal spiritual power and intention into it. Oils can be used on their own to purify ritual tools or bless oneself or another person for a particular purpose. They can also be used in tandem with other rituals and spells. Along with being a sealant, oils accelerate and intensify the spiritual energies at work.

Because oils are so potent, they are a must for any Hoodoo practitioner looking to take control of their life through the spiritual. However, it means that it can be difficult to make your own oils as a beginner as there is a lot to keep in mind when creating oils. You have to have clear intention and a strong grasp of the intricacies of the different herbs. An understanding and connection with rootwork are a must if you intend to make your own oils.

We'll be including recipes for making holy oils. To make holy oil, you'll need a base oil that is safe to apply to the skin, such as coconut, grapeseed, sunflower, jojoba, safflower, or almond. The rest of your oils will be concentrated essential oils which can be dangerous to apply directly on the skin. You'll want to use an eyedropper to add these oils into the base and store your final mixture in a sealed glass. It's important to make sure your essential oils are pure and undiluted. It's easy to confuse real essential oils with perfumes so seek out Grade A or therapeutic grade oil. If you don't feel ready or if you don't have the resources to make your own oils, don't worry. There are several common and useful oils that you can find premade by experienced Hoodoo practitioners. Many sacred Hoodoo oils go back to the birth of Hoodoo and have served generations upon generations.

Some recipes will have specific measurements, and some will have general ratios or 'parts,' which refer to whichever kind of unit of measurement you choose based on the batch size (e.g., one 'part' could be a drop of oil, an ounce, a whole cup, or a gram of ground herbs — whichever applies to your case). Beware that resins and ground herbs will be more concentrated than freshly harvested ingredients of the same type.

Abramelin Oils

Abramelin Oil is one of the oldest and most commonly used conjuring oils. It is a type of Holy Jewish Oil described in Exodus in the Bible. Much of its power in Judaism comes from the symbolic importance of each ingredient. The base oil of the recipe is olive oil, representing of happiness, domesticity, and God's Wisdom. Myrrh represents sacredness and great contemplation of the universe. Cinnamon invokes warmth and

Calamus invokes masculinity and love. Some recipes will also include a galangal, representing oneness.

In Hoodoo, the symbolism is somewhat different. Cinnamon represents good luck and prosperity, calamus represents protection from the evil eye, and galangal offers overall protection.

Recipe 1

You'll need: 7 parts olive oil, 1 part ground calamus root, 2 parts ground myrrh resin, 4 parts ground cinnamon bark, and a dark glass container.

- Step One: Swirl the powders into the oil clockwise.

- Step Two: Let the mixture sit in a sealed glass container in a cool, dark place for a month before using.

Recipe 2

You'll need: 7 parts olive oil, 1 part cassia essential oil, ½ part cinnamon essential oil, 1 part myrrh essential oil, 1 part calamus essential oil, and a glass bottle.

- Step One: Add the essential oils into the olive oil and stir clockwise.

- Step Two: Store in a sealed glass bottle and store in a cool, dark place.

Recipe 3

You'll need: 7 parts olive oil, 4 pieces of cinnamon bark (ground), 1 part ground galangal root, 2 pieces of ground myrrh resin, and a glass bottle.

- Step One: Add the powder into the olive oil and stir clockwise.

- Step Two: Pour the mixture into a glass bottle and let it sit for a month.

- Step Three: Filter the mixture through a tumbler to remove the sediment.

- Step Four: Store in a sealed glass bottle in a cool, dark place.

Confusion Oil

Confusion oil, as the name suggests, is used to create confusion and instability in those who are trying to harm you or cause you strife. It will disrupt their ability to curse you and can divert curses already cast.

You'll need: 2 ounces grapeseed oil, 1 full dropper essential marjoram oil, 2 full droppers patchouli essential oil, 1 full dropper vetiver essential oil, 2 teaspoons grains of paradise, 2 teaspoons black mustard seed, 2 teaspoons poppy seed, and a glass bottle.

- Step One: Grind the black mustard seed, poppy seed, and grains of paradise into a fine powder.

- Step Two: Add the essential oils into the powder.

- Step Three: Add the mixture into the grapeseed and stir clockwise until well incorporated.

- Step Four: Pour the mixture into a sealed glass bottle and store it in a cool, dark place.

Altar Oil

Altar oil is a sort of all-purpose holy oil that can be used to anoint and bless your altar and ritual items. It can be used to call upon your deities to help you at your altar.

You'll need: 2 ounces olive oil, 1 drop cedar essential oil, 4 drops frankincense essential oil, 2 drops myrrh essential oils, and a glass bottle.

- Step One: Add the essential oils into the olive oil and swirl clockwise.

- Step Two: Pour the mixture into a glass bottle and store it in a cool, dark place.

Uncrossing Oil

Uncrossing oil can be used to sever negative connections. It can reverse spells, ward off evil spirits, and protect you from the evil eye. You can also use it to revert curses back to their sender.

You'll need: 2 ounces almond essential oil, 2 drops clove essential oil, 2 drops vetiver essential oil, and a glass bottle.

- Step One: Mix the essential oils together and stir clockwise.

- Step Two: Add the mixture into the almond oil and stir clockwise.

- Step Three: Pour the mixture into a glass bottle and store it in a cool, dark place.

Fast Luck Oil

Fast luck oil will help you find good luck in all aspects of your life. It invites the favor of your deities and ancestors and increases the power of rituals and spells that reflect your desire for greater things. Whether it's money, love, business, or school, fast luck oil will help attract good things.

You'll need: One ounce sunflower oil, 1 drop cinnamon essential oil, 2 drops rosemary essential oil, 2 drops lemon essential oil, 2 drops dragon's blood essential oil, and a glass bottle.

- Step One: Mix the essential oils together and stir clockwise.

- Step Two: Add the mixture into the sunflower oil and

stir clockwise.

- Step Three: Pour the mixture into a glass bottle and store in a cool, dark place.

Love Attraction Oil

Use this oil in any spell relating to love and romance. Whether you're trying to woo someone, rekindle an existing relationship, or achieve more romantic and sexual confidence, love oil can help you.

You'll need: 12 rose petals, a sprig of peppermint, a sprig of parsley, 3 cinnamon-basil leaves, ½ tsp. caraway seeds, ½ tsp. rosemary, ½ tsp. yarrow, ½ tsp. catnip, ½ tsp. cloves, 6 drops orange essential oil, 6 drops jasmine essential oil, 6 drops lemon essential oil, 6 drops rose essential oil, 6 drops vanilla essential oil, lavender buds, a red glass bottle, and enough olive oil to fill the bottle ¾ of the way.

- Step One: Grind the caraway seeds, cloves, rosemary, yarrow, and catnip into a fine powder.

- Step Two: Put the powder into the red glass bottle and fill it up ¾ of the way with olive oil.

- Step Three: Add the essential oils and stir clockwise.

- Step Four: Fill the bottle the rest of the way up with lavender buds. Seal and store in a cool, dark place.

Van Van Oil

This traditional Hoodoo conjure oil is used to protect from evil. It acts as a barrier that turns bad luck into good and can enhance spells and rituals related to strength and protection.

You'll need: 1 ounce almond oil, 8 full droppers lemongrass essential oil, ½ dropper ginger grass essential oil, ½ dropper palmarosa essential oil, ½ dropper vetiver oil, 4 full droppers citronella oil, 1 pinch dried lemongrass leaves, 1 pinch crushed pyrite, and a glass bottle.

- Step One: Mix the essential oils together and allow them to sit for a week.

- Step Two: Add the pyrite, lemongrass leaves, and a full dropper of the essential oil mix into the almond oil and stir clockwise. Save the essential oil mix to make more as needed.

- Step Three: Pour into a glass bottle and pour in a cool, dark place.

Come to Me Oil

This oil will help you draw attention. Whether you're looking to find a new lover or if you have a particular person in mind, you can use this oil to make yourself impossible to ignore, and intensify your love spells. This can also work on non-romantic relationships, like friends and family you've lost touch with.

You'll need: 1 ounce grapeseed oil, ½ dropper patchouli essential oil, 1 drop ginger essential oil, 6 drops jasmine essential oil, 7 drops cinnamon essential oil, a piece of cinnamon stick, and a glass bottle.

- Step One: Add essential oils into the grapeseed oil and stir clockwise.

- Step Two: Pour the mixture into a glass bottle and store it in a cool, dark place.

All Saints Oil

This oil calls upon the spirits to act on your behalf. It helps facilitate healing, attract success and blessings, and open your spiritual communication. It's particularly powerful when working with the Catholic Saints, though practitioners of any religion will find this oil powerful.

You'll need: 1 ounce almond oil, ½ tsp. patchouli oil, ½ dropper vetiver oil, ½ dropper gardenia oil, ½ dropper rose essential oil, ½ dropper cinnamon essential oil, 1 whole vanilla bean, and a glass bottle.

- Step One: Crush the vanilla bean into a powder.

- Step Two: Add the powder and essential oils into the almond oil. Stir clockwise.

- Step Three: Pour the mixture into a glass bottle and store it in a cool, dark place.

Anointing Oil

This basic formula is perfect for blessing and anointing yourself and your ritual tools, making it the perfect oil to keep on your altar.

You'll need: 1 ounce olive oil, 35 drops frankincense essential oil, 35 drops myrrh essential oil, and a glass bottle.

- Step One: Mix the essential oil into the olive oil and stir clockwise.

- Step Two: Pour the mixture into the glass bottle and store it in a cool, dark place.

Attraction Oil

Attraction oil acts as a magnet in your life. It can make you more attractive to potential lovers, but its power extends past romance. Use this oil to draw your desires towards you and open the door to new and positive experiences. It will enhance the result of any spell related to the things you want.

You'll need: 2 ounces almond oil, equal parts lovage herb and lemon peel or lemon flowers, a piece of magnetite, and a glass bottle.

- Step One: Grind the lovage and lemon peel or flowers into a powder.

- Step Two: Add the mixture into the almond oil and stir clockwise.

- Step Three: Place the magnetite into the glass bottle and pour in the mixture. Store in a cool, dark place.

Crown of Success Oil

Crown of Success oil will help you accomplish your goals. It can be used to break down barriers to your goals and give you an advantage in all your endeavors.

You'll need: 1 ounce olive oil, ½ tsp. sandalwood essential oil, ½ tsp. copal essential oil, ½ tsp. vetiver essential oil, ½ tsp. bay leaf, ½ tsp. aloeswood, and a glass bottle.

- Step One: Grind the bay leaf and aloeswood into a fine powder.

- Step Two: Add the powder and the essential oils into the olive oil and stir clockwise.

- Step Three: Pour the mixture into a glass bottle and store it in a dark, cool place.

Master Key Oil

This oil is so named due to its ability to unlock doors and open barriers in one's life. It frees someone's magical and spiritual abilities, and can help you gain control over a situation.

You'll need: 2 ounces almond oil, ¼ tsp. vanilla bean, ¼ tsp. vervain, ¼ tsp. star anise, ¼ tsp. sage, ¼ tsp. patchouli, ¼ tsp. myrrh, ¼ tsp. galangal root, ¼ tsp. frankincense, ¼ tsp. cinnamon, ¼ tsp. master root, a small key, and a glass bottle.

- Step One: Grind the herbs into a fine powder.

- Step Two: Add one teaspoon of the powder mixture into the almond oil and stir clockwise. Save the rest of the powder to make more as needed.

- Step Three: Place the small key at the bottom of the glass bottle.

- Step Four: Pour the mixture into the glass bottle and store it in a cool, dark place.

How to Use Oils

Oils can help intensify your goals and add power to your intentions. For example, you can dab a small amount of an appropriate oil onto a job application before you send it in to communicate to the spirits your desire. You can also do this with your ritual tools, such as your altar table or conjure. Place a small bit of an appropriate oil on your tools while speaking a prayer about your goals and intentions. Conure oils are also used to feed ritual items that lose their power over time, such as mojo bags or Hoodoo dolls, which we will discuss later.

Physical Anointing

Oil can be used to affect people directly if they are properly made and safe to apply on the skin. Love oils may be rubbed over the heart. Attraction oils are often placed on pulse points so that the smell is more notable.

If you're trying to affect another person without their knowledge, you'll want to place the oil somewhere you know they'll come into contact with, such as a doorknob or doorway they regularly walk through. While placing the oil onto the area, speak their name out loud and make your intentions known. This way, the spell will only affect the desired target.

You can also make powders from crushed herb mixtures and use these where oils would be inconvenient or impractical. You can sprinkle these powders around an area to get the desired effect.

Dressing Candles

When doing candle spells, which we will discuss in more detail, you'll want to first dress your candle, also known as fixing. This purifies the candle and seals your intention and its spiritual power into the candle until it is burned out.

To dress a candle, hold it with the base towards your belly button. Dip your fingers into your powder or oil.

If the goal of your spell is to repel something, rub your finger from the base to the tip. If the goal is to bring something towards you, rub your finger from tip to base. After this, you can roll the candle in an herb mixture consistent with your goals.

Conclusion

Oils can be used at any level in Hoodoo. They can help facilitate a spell and create a conducive environment for conjuring, help access your spiritual power, or used as spells on their own to help you easily achieve your goals. When you have a steady collection of oils, you can access the spiritual daily and give yourself the boost you need.

CHAPTER 4

Candle Magic

Many of the most powerful Hoodoo spells require an aspect of candle burning. However, the importance of candles is not unique to Hoodoo. Candles hold significance in nearly all societies across the globe. They represent the distillation of man's greatest achievement: conquering fire. Candles follow human society and progress. Even without context, lit candles evoke a sense of spirituality.

Why Candles Work

There are many theories as to why candles have spiritual significance that differ from culture to culture. For example, philosopher Gaston Bachelard viewed candles as a representation of unity, a literal example of the illumination or enlightenment that we seek spiritually. In England, candles were burned on All Sant's Eve to protect against witches and black magic. Lighting candles at birthdays comes from the belief that the flame will protect the child from evil spirits. There are some core truths about candles that can be seen throughout different beliefs.

Focus and Intent

Candles are often used in meditation practices. The light itself provides a singular point of focus that can help keep the mind focused. The soft lighting also helps create a calm atmosphere. When practicing Hoodoo, candles can help you stay grounded in the present moment and focused on the task at hand. Intention is incredibly important to spellcasting. A wandering mind can get in the way of your spiritual power. No matter how knowledgeable you are about the tools and practice of Hoodoo, without a steady focused mind, you won't be successful. It might be difficult to stay focused in the beginning. However, with practice, intent and focus will get easier and you will carry that inner peace and clarity into your daily life.

Not only does the candle help you with the spiritual power of focus, but the simple act of spell casting or the candle you chose will represent your goals. Everything about the candle, including color, shape, and scent, can and should express your goals. By returning your eyes and mind to the candle, you are constantly aware of your goals and intensify the results.

Beacons

The light of a candle acts as a beacon that can guide the spirits and deities to you to aid your ability and give power to your intentions.

Candles are the combination of the four elements; wax represents water, the flame represents fire, the oxygen that feeds the flame represents air, and the wick represents Earth.

The candle brings them all together along with the other magical elements in the ritual. As the smoke rises, your wishes are sent to those who have the spiritual power to assist you. While we may think of the candle as one thing, there are many different elements of a candle that can be customized to a specific goal.

What Candle Do You Use?

Many of the most basic candles used in Hoodoo can be found in any witchcraft store, specifically Jewish spiritualist stores, as many early Hoodoo practitioners borrowed some cultural practices from the Jewish people, especially in urban areas. As natural items are always going to be your best bet, choose candles that are made of a natural substance like beeswax, soy wax, or palm wax. You'll want to avoid artificial waxes, such as paraffin. Natural waxes are also biodegradable which will allow you to burn the candle after the ritual and give back to the Earth in thanks.

You'll also want to avoid scented candles for the most part. The herbs or artificial perfumes can create conflicting energy that will get in the way of your spellcasting. Some Hoodoo candles are scented, but they are scented with natural herbs mixed for a particular purpose.

Color

There is power in color. Color is how we understand the unique vibrations of light around us. Color affects our moods and holds deep associations that can help us focus our goals and intent.

Black Candles

Despite common assumptions, black doesn't necessarily mean evil. In Hoodoo, black signifies protection and dominance. These candles should be used in spells seeking to fight back against curses, the evil eye, or danger. It can also help you build up your personal strength and assert dominance over a person or situation.

White Candles

White is the color of purification and purity, and it protects by dispelling evil. White is calming and can evoke a deep sense of tranquility and spiritual awareness. It is also used as a neutral color that can be used for any type of spell. You can also choose a white candle if you're struggling to achieve mental clarity.

Orange Candles

Orange provides energy and stimulation. Orange can enhance a person's wit and mental quickness. If you're struggling with indecision or looking to take action in your life, use an orange candle.

Yellow Candles

Yellow is an energetic and cerebral color that attracts joy and can brighten the darkest of moods. Yellow candles are great for spells dealing with depression, grief, or sadness. They can help you overcome brain fog and enhance your creativity and logical thought. They can also help bring joy to friendships.

Gold Candles

Gold is a masculine color and can be used to enhance male energy and potency. It is also a royal and enlightened color. Use gold candles when you want to call upon or address God or when seeking confidence, prosperity, wisdom, and power.

Blue Candles

Blue is a calm and cooling color, and can help offset anxiety or panic. It is also associated with physical, spiritual, and emotional healing, and is therefore great for healing spells. It is especially great for dealing with mental health. Light blue candles inspire the mind and enhance focus and prophetic ability. Royal blue candles can help you connect with the spiritual realm and your own spiritual power.

Pink Candles

Pink is the color of innocent and romantic love. It can be used in matters of affection and friendship, and can also help attract general love into your life. Whether you're seeking to love yourself or your life circumstances or if you'd like to share more love with the people around you, you can reach for a pink candle. Darker shades of pink, such as magenta, are more flirtatious and related to romantic confidence.

Brown Candles

By using the color of the Earth, you can use candle magic to ground yourself and find harmony between your physical and spiritual self. This color is associated with balance, neutrality, and objectivity and can be used if you're struggling to find your footing in a difficult situation or when you're facing a difficult situation. It is also associated with deep connections and trust, and can be used when dealing with relationships.

Purple Candles

Purple is the color of the crown chakra, located on the top of the head. The crown chakra is said to connect our physical bodies to the spiritual world by a sort of umbilical cord that breaks when we die. Purple candles can help you access the divine. They are great when seeking prophecy, spiritual wisdom, or enlightenment. They can also help you tap into your natural royalty and divinity. If you're looking to walk in confidence and achieve success and independence, purple candles can do the trick.

Green Candles

As you might suspect, green represents wealth and prosperity, as well as good luck. Green is the color of plants and vegetation and can help you achieve growth throughout your life. Burning a green candle will help you achieve abundance, good health, and can even be used for fertility spells.

Red Candles

Red is the color of passion and adds vibrance, intensity, and energy to spells. It is associated with intense emotions, making these spells particularly powerful, if somewhat dangerous. It may take extra effort and clarity to keep your mind focused and your emotions in check when doing these spells to avoid chaos and harm. Red is the color of love, and is distinct from pink in that it taps into a more sensual and sexual love. Red candles can intensify your passion, make you more attractive, and boost your sexual prowess. They can also help you tap into your personal strength.

Silver Candles

Silver is associated with the moon and thus femininity. Silver candles can be used to tap into your divine feminine energy. Silver candles also create a light similar to that of moonlight, and can be used in place of natural light for spells that call for moonlight. Silver also helps you tap into your intuition and can inspire prophetic dreams.

Hoodoo Candles

There are several types of candles that you can use in your rituals. The size, shape, and burn time of a candle are important when choosing which candle to use. In addition to common candle shapes, there are also specific Hoodoo candles made with specific oils and herb blends to help you achieve a specific purpose.

Taper Candles

Taper candles are tall, thin candles that need to be supported by a candleholder. Taper candles burn for about an hour per inch depending on what they're made of. These are commonly used for specific candle spells.

Pillar Candles

These are large, cylindrical candles that don't require a candle holder, though you may want to place it on a plate or in a glass to catch the dripping wax. They come in a variety of sizes. On average, they burn for about 3–4 hours, and are usually smokeless. These are great options to keep burning on your altar to keep a constant beacon of light going as well as for specific spells.

Votive Candles

Votives are very small, usually 2x2 inches, and require a holder. They are commonly used in churches. Despite their size, they can burn for 6–7 hours. You can keep several votives on your altar at once to keep a soft glow of light.

Tealights

Tealights, also known as tea candles, are small and lightweight. They are similar to votive candles, but shorter and burn faster, usually within 2–3 hours.

Double Action Candles

Double action candles combine two different colors of wax to double the results of your spell and deliver fast results. While one color draws something towards you, the other drives the negative forces away.

Black/White candles can drive away spells and curses and provide protection. Black/Red candles address love problems by dispelling any obstacles that might be getting in the way and attract love and strong relationships. Black/Green candles remove financial barriers and attract prosperity. Black with Red inside send curses back to their sender.

Human Figure Candles

As the name suggests, these are candles made in the shape of people, either male or female. These are used to represent the person you're focusing your spell on.

Skull Candles

Skull candles are used to target the mind. For example, a white skull may be used to provide clarity, while a red skull might create passion or intense emotions. Some people also use these candles to address health problems or curse others.

Cat Candles

Cat-shaped candles are used to attract good luck, as cats are known for their ability to always land on their feet.

Genital Candles

Candles shaped like genitals are used in spells related to sexual health and wellness, as well as attraction. They can be used to attract a sexual partner or affect an existing sexual relationship.

Adam and Eve Candle

These candles combine oils and herbs such as patchouli, lemongrass, and lavender to help bring a couple closer. They are often used for spells relating to marriage and fidelity. You can also find an Alice and Eve and Adam and Steve candles for dealing with same-sex couples.

Come To Me

Whether you're looking to attract a specific love interest or simply make yourself more attractive and open to romantic situations, this candle can help you attract real love or reignite a spark to an existing relationship.

Crown of Glory

This candle will help you achieve success and victory in all things.

Stop Gossip Candle

Use this candle to stop the spread of rumors and the harm they cause. It can also help heal the damage done by gossip, and protect you from social attacks.

High John Candle

This candle invokes the divine masculine energy. It can be used in spells related to overcoming and taking control of any obstacle. It invokes power, stamina, and dominance.

Lucky 7 Candle

This warm, spiced candle helps attract good luck and fortune. Use it when you need a boost to push you towards success, such as before an audition or test. It's specifically useful to achieve success in games and gambling.

Money Draw Candle

Use this candle to attract wealth to meet all your wants and needs.

Seven-Day Candle

These are commonly known as seven knob candles. There are seven different sections that can be burned each day for any spells that are done over the course of a week.

Spiritual Cleansing Candle

These candles are white and made with lemongrass, cypress, and sage. Use this to cleanse your space and mind of negativity. They can be used to deal with negative self-talk, poor mental health, or spiritual blocks.

Steady Job Candle

This earthy, minty candle is used to attract prosperity in your workplace, help you get a new job, and protect your employment.

Tranquil Home Candle

This lavender, floral candle is used to bring calm to a situation. It can be used to address arguments and conflicts, as well as bless and protect a new home.

Uncrossing Candle

This candle will help break any bonds or negativity that are holding you back, just like Uncrossing Oil.

How To Do Candle Spells

Now that you know which candle will be best to get what you want out of your spell, you can start the ritual. The first thing you should always do is cleanse your altar with smoke or oil to make sure you've created the most spiritually active and positive space. With the space prepared, seal your intentions into the candle.

Light some incense or candles to help you focus. Take the candle and hold it close to your heart while you meditate and pray over the candle. Imagine your thoughts flowing down through your body and into the candle. Focus on what you want out of your spell, how you want it to manifest, who you want it to affect, etc. You can also carve a name or symbols into your candle to further set your intention. When you're comfortable that your intention has been placed, set the candle down on the altar or into a candle holder and light it. It's best to use a wooden matchstick as it's more natural, but a lighter is fine.

Cup your hands around the fire and once again meditate on your intent while you focus on the flame. You can use this time to read out psalms or speak your prayers out loud, however you feel it's best to communicate with the spirits. After this, let the candle burn all the way out as most spells encourage not blowing out the candle.

These are the basics of candle spells. By using this system, you can customize and create a specific candle spell for any purpose. If you're still struggling to get the result you want out of your candle spells, you may want to try a ritual specifically meant to enhance your access to your spiritual ability.

Candle Spells for Love

This spell can be intensified by adding herbs like cinnamon, apple, rose, or sandalwood in the form of incense or burning in your cauldron. Think of what you'd specifically want out of this spell. For example, you may want to love yourself better, or heal the strife in your relationship.

Whatever the case, hold the candle to your heart and speak the words, "Creature of wax and wick, please help me in _____" then say your wish.

Repeat this with the beginning phrases, "Creature of earth and grass please help me in _____," "Creature of stone and bone please help me in _____."

As you light the candle, say, "Fire creature lease light this flame and help me in _____"

Focus on your good qualities - all the things that make you lovable - while you sit with your candle for 15–20 minutes, or until you feel at peace that your spell has been heard. You may also want to stay in the room with the candle until it burns out so you can continue to bask in its light.

Candle Spells for Protection and Healing

Enhance this spell with apples, flowers, or the sound of running water. Light a candle on your altar. Wash some stones in running water and form a circle around yourself to form a comforting, womb-like environment. You can also draw the circle with oil or powder. Set up your circle in a clockwise position while focusing on the fact that you are making a space for healing. Stay inside the circle as you create it.

To start your healing process, purge your negative emotions and the things ailing you. There are many ways you can do this. Whether you choose to allow yourself to cry, go through progressive relaxation, write your emotions and burn the pages, or simply engage in breathe-focused meditation, allow yourself to let go of the things you need to heal from.

Once this is done, focus on the flame. Imagine its light flowing through your head and into your body, spreading its healing light all the way through you. Once you feel relieved and satisfied with the results, you can break the circle. If you use stones, carry one of these with you as a totem of your healing session. If the candle has not burned out, you can use the same candle to repeat the ritual over the next few days to continue the healing process.

Candle Spell for Prosperity

Surround yourself with things that make you feel rich and abundant. This can include luxurious clothes, treasured items, or things that bring you a sense of joy and wholeness. Light an appropriate candle and cup your hands around the flame to form a connection with it. Focus on what you desire.

What areas of your life are lacking? What would a life of absolute abundance look like to you? Speak these desires in great detail over the candle's flame until you have expressed all of your deepest feelings and desires.

After this, close your eyes and allow yourself to enter the abundant, prosperous life you desire. You can also write down your thoughts and desires. Once you're done, blow out the candle and visualize all the dreams you've expressed flowing into you. You can also repeat this until your candle is fully burned out.

Candle Spell for Clarity of the Mind

For this spell, you'll want a bowl of water, something to write with, and a fan or feather. You can also include lemons, lemongrass, feathers, or cardamon in your ritual. Light your candle and ask for the mental clarity you desire. Sit down and meditate. As thoughts come into your mind, write them down to acknowledge them and then let them go. Focus on the water and the candle. The feather or fan can be used to help you visualize blowing stray thoughts away.

Once you've done this for 20–30 minutes or until your mind feels clear, tear up what you've written so that each different thought is on a different piece. Starting with the most harmful thought, burn each one. As you do, your negative thoughts will also be burned away. Examine the last 1–3 pieces and consider if these are something you want to hold onto or not. If not, burn them as well. As you allow the candle to burn, imagine the space being purified of all the negative thoughts that have plagued you. Repeat this every week or so until the candle is burned out.

Candle Divination

The behavior of the candle flame can reveal a lot about the context and efficacy of your spell. To get accurate information based on the movement of your flame, you'll want to perform your spells somewhere without a draft or breeze so that it isn't disrupted by external sources. By paying attention to your flame behavior, you can avoid making mistakes in your spell and get the best results possible.

Jumping Flame

If your flame is jumping and moving about, this is the first sign of some sort of opposition or obstacle standing in the way of your spell.

High Flame

A high flame means the spell is working powerfully and quickly.

This is a sign that you have communicated well with the spirits and taken the proper steps in your spell.

Low Flame

Your spell isn't working the way it should. This could mean many things. It could be that you have not properly cleansed your space, yourself, or your tools and that negative energy is interfering with the spell. It could also mean that an enemy is trying to curse you or that they are covered by a veil of protection too strong for you to penetrate at the time. Either way, you need to do some other ritual and review whether you completed the current ritual correctly.

White Smoke

If there is white smoke, you will get what you want, but it won't be without difficulty.

Black Smoke at First

Black smoke is the candle burning away the negative energy. When the black smoke stops, this means your candle spell has succeeded in dispelling the negative energy.

Lots of Black Smoke

If the black smoke persists, you do not have the power to overcome the negative energy. You may need to cleanse. If you're doing a spell against someone, you risk intensifying their curse against you or causing harm to yourself so you should stop the spell immediately.

Partial Flame

Your spell will work but it is weak, and you'll only get some of what you asked for.

Multiple Flames

The central flame is you, while any other flames represent people working against you. In a love ritual, the other flame might represent a rival. In an offensive spell, it may represent your enemy's allies, physical or spiritual.

Candle Catches on Fire

There are large obstacles in your way, probably because you didn't do some part of the ritual correctly and the spiritual energy is not moving and working as it should. If this is an offensive spell, it might mean your enemy knows you are working against them.

Flickering

Your spell has been done correctly but is not strong enough. You may need to step back, cleanse and work on building your spiritual power and communication with the spirits before trying again.

Crackling

The pops represent some sort of opposition or struggle against you. The louder the pops, the stronger the power of those working against you.

Conclusion

Candles are a simple, yet powerful way to establish communication between the physical and the spiritual realm. Since magic is the connection of these two things, candles are a necessity, especially if you struggle with keeping your focus and using the full power of your intentions in your conjuring. Candle magic is nearly ubiquitous across folk magic practices so you can find them easily at any witchcraft shop or even local farmer's market.

With a good understanding of the different types of candles, the meanings of each color, and how to handle and use your candle, you can start accessing the spiritual and working on your own behalf.

CHAPTER 5

Mojo Bags and Hoodoo Dolls

Ritual magic is great for expressing your wishes and taking care of your spiritual self. However, it can feel like you're left out on your own after the ritual is done and you have to return to your life. Magical items give you a physical reminder of the magic you've done, something that constantly holds that power on your behalf. These items, things like magic pendants, wands, and charms are what most people think of when they imagine magic. While there is a lot of misinformation about the items, there is a truth to the power magical items can possess.

What Is a Mojo Bag?

Mojo bags, also known as gris-gris bags, are an ancient magical practice from West Africa. They are a talisman that is carried on the body to provide magical power for various purposes. You can make a mojo bag to fulfill any personal need, such as attracting love, physical protection, or maintaining strength.

Whereas spells are requests that send the spirits on specific errands, mojo bags go beyond that. In many ways, they are more than just talismans. They are living, invested spiritual allies, a friend, and protector that you carry around and communicate with as you move through your life. They are tied to your soul, your future, and all your desires. Just like individuals, there is no limit to the uniqueness of each Mojo bag.

Material

Mojo bags are the combination of all the tools and powers of Hoodoo. Everything from herbs, to oils, to color magic, to charms, comes together with the power of the spirits and the conjurer's intent to create these powerful talismans.

The first ingredient you need is cloth to form the outside of the mojo bag. For the bag, you'll want to use a natural fiber such as cotton or wool. Use color theory to express your desires for your mojo bag. For example, a black bag is meant to protect you and enhance your dominant energy, while green is meant to attract wealth and prosperity. You can buy a premade drawstring bag, or you can sew the bag closed yourself.

You'll then need to fill the mojo bag with magical items. Think of these as the organs of the bag. Many people add an odd number of items to their bags. This can include herbs, stones, coins, bones, or other curios with spiritual significance. You may also want to include your own taglock.

A 'taglock' is something that holds a connection to a specific person. This is usually a piece of the body, such as hair or fingernails. However, a piece of clothing or a picture can also work as a taglock. The more items the mojo bag has, the more powerful it will be, as long as they are in harmony with each other. One mojo bag cannot be made to address every single issue in one's life, so you don't want to include conflicting energies.

Creating and Taking Care of Your Mojo Bag

Make your mojo bag at a purified and cleansed altar. You may also want to burn candles or burn incense to make sure the spirits are moving. As you place the items into your mojo bag and start sewing it together, think about the name you want to give your mojo bag. As a mojo bag is a living being, it has to have a name. You can elect to let the bag itself give itself a name by meditating on the issue or letting it come to you in a dream. You can also name your mojo bag after someone who represents your goals and desires or simply give it a name that's meaningful to you.

Now that your bag is named, speak it out loud. Use the name to address the bag and talk to it about what you're asking of it. Your bag should be carried under your clothes against your skin and below the waist. For the first week of its life, sleep next to your mojo bag to enhance your connection. After that, you can store it somewhere private or continue to sleep next to it.

Mojo bags need to be fed to keep them alive and well. Just like a body needs calories, your mojo bag needs a steady supply of spiritually energy. You can feed your bag with spiritual oils, incense, holy waters, liquors, powders, or even bodily fluids. To feed your bag, dip your finger into the oil or holy water and dab it onto the bag five times in the same configuration as the "five" side of a dice. You can also dab it in a star pattern. Make sure to only use a small amount of oil each time so your mojo bag doesn't get soggy. To feed your bag with incense, hold the lit incense in one hand and the mojo bag in the other. Wave the incense stick around the bag so that the bag is fully engulfed in smoke. You can also say a prayer asking the spirits to help reenergize your mojo bag as you feed it. Make sure to feed your bag at least once a week.

While you can use any holy oils or powders to feed your bag, you can strengthen your mojo bag by being specific with what you use to feed it. You'll also bring the energy of your intent into the feeding oil or powder when you make it with your own hands. Feel free to create your own recipes with your herbal knowledge according to your specific desires. These are just a few quick and easy suggestions for common types of mojo bags.

- Powder for money: Grind up High John the Conqueror Root and cloves into a fine powder. Add a few drops of chamomile essential oil.

- Powder for protection: Grind up sage and tobacco into a fine powder. Add a few drops of van van oil.

- Powder for love: Grind patchouli and orris root into a fine powder. Add a few drops of vanilla oil.

- Oil for power: Add four drops of orange essential oil, 1 drop of ginger essential oil, and 1 drop of pine oil into an ounce of olive oil or other base oil.

- Oil for love: Add one drop of lavender oil, one drop of orange oil, one drop of rose oil, one drop of cinnamon oil, and one drop of ylang ylang oil into an ounce of olive oil or other base oil.

- Oil/powder for courage: Grind rosemary, gardenia petals, High John the Conqueror Root, and five finger grass into a fine powder. You can use this mixture alone or add two tablespoons into 2 ounces of olive oil.

If you keep in tune with your mojo bag, you'll feel its strength and energy. A mojo bag will begin to weaken after a year. If it still has life after this time, you can sew the ingredients of the mojo bag into a new cloth to refresh it. However, a mojo bag can also die after a time if not properly cared for and refreshed.

It can also be killed if someone sees it.

If someone sees your mojo bag and you feel it is still alive but weakened, you can try to revive it with rose or geranium water. However, if this doesn't work, you should give your mojo bag a proper burial.

Mojo Bag Recipes

While your mojo bag should be personalized and speak to your spirit, here are a few ideas that help guide you in making your mojo bag.

Attraction

- Base: A red or pink flannel bag

- Herbs: Tonka bean, lovage root, passionflower, lavender, spikenard, gentian root, coriander seed, licorice root, roses, violet, catnip, Spanish saffron, damiana leaf, lovage root

- To Feed Your Bag: Sugar, three king's incense, love me oil

- Other: Your taglock, the taglock of the person you want to attract, the seal of Venus on a paper or pendant, a pair of lodestones, dirt from a wedding chapel

Fill the bag with everything except the incense and oils. Tie it at the neck and waft the smoke from the three king's incense over the bag while you speak Psalm 65. Feed the bag with the love me oil. Place the bag on your skin and under your mattress while you sleep for the next week.

Money

- Base: A red or green flannel bag

- Herbs: Buckeye, cinnamon clove, silverweed, five finger grass

- To Feed Your Bag: Money drawing oil, money drawing incense

- Other: A pair of lodestones, a coin

Fill the bag with everything except the incense and oil. Smoke with money drawing incense while praying Psalm 65. Feed the bag with the money drawing oil. Wear it against your skin. When you aren't wearing it, hide it under your mattress.

Good Health

- Base: A red or green flannel bag

- Herbs: Cayenne, Eucalyptus, rosemary, rose petals

- To Feed Your Bag: Health oil, health incense

- Other: Your own taglock

Fill the bag with everything except the oil and incense. Smoke the bag with the health incense while speaking Psalm 30 over it. Wear it against your skin during the day and hide under your mattress at night.

Business

- Base: A green bag

- Herbs: St. Joseph beans, alkanet root, Irish moss, cinnamon chips

- To Feed Your Bag: Better business oil, three kings incense

- Other: Your business card, money, a lodestone, pyrite, dirt from a successful local business or bank

Fill the bag with everything except the oil and incense. Smoke the bag with the incense while speaking Psalm 114 over it, then feed the bag with the oil. During your regular business hours, wear the bag against your skin or put it in the register.

What Is a Hoodoo Doll?

Hoodoo dolls are the most misunderstood part of Hoodoo and rootwork practice and culture. It conjures images of creepy dolls full of pins meant to harm people with absurd specificity. In reality, Hoodoo dolls can be used for a variety of purposes and while harm can certainly be one, they're most often used to add goodness in the life of a person.

The idea that you can change something by manipulating an image or fabrication of it goes back to the paleolithic era, and is present in many belief systems. This works off the concept of sympathetic magic, which states that all things are bonded by invisible ties; homeopathic magic, which states that like things attract one another; and contagious magic, which states that once two things come into contact, they are forever bonded. Hoodoo dolls utilize these concepts to create a physical manifestation of a person or spirit that can be directly interacted with to create the desired outcome.

Types of Hoodoo Dolls

There are four main types of Hoodoo dolls, categorized by what they represent and how they function.

The first is **spirit dolls**. Think of these as the grounded equivalent of the haunted doll trope. Spirit dolls hold a specific spirit. This can be someone deceased or a divine being or deity. People often used spirit dolls to directly engage with spirits that are important to their practice. The dolls typically sit at the altar and receive offerings and prayers.

The second type are called **helper dolls**. The dolls act as physical manifestations of a particular concept or goal. For example, you may have a money helper doll or a love helper doll. They are very similar to mojo bags in that they are consistent allies working with you towards a goal. Unlike spirit dolls, they do not hold a specific pre-existing spirit or soul.

The last two dolls are **doll-babies** and **effigies**. These are closest to the media representation of Hoodoo dolls. They are meant to represent a particular living person and are built to evoke and resemble that person as much as possible. Doll-babies are made to represent other people, whereas effigies are meant to represent the conjurer. These dolls can be used to any effect, such as good health, love, or strength. How you interact with the doll will dictate how the person is affected.

As far as sticking pins into the dolls, while it is certainly possible to cause someone harm by how you treat their doll baby, it is not nearly as direct as stabbing the doll and causing them a stabbing sensation. You must also keep in mind that, if you are not fairly and justly trying to punish someone for some wrongdoing, what you're doing may be considered black magic — which can endanger you as well.

Making a Hoodoo Doll

There are three main ways to make a Hoodoo doll. The first is to buy a doll that reminds you of the person or entity you're trying to invoke. You'll need to clean and cleanse the doll and include as many personal effects as possible. You might stuff some of the person's hair or fingernails into the doll, recolor its eyes to match the target, or dress it in clothes that evoke the target. This is the easier way to make a Hoodoo doll, but you will end up sacrificing some specificity.

You can also use human figure candles as Hoodoo dolls. This is especially useful for combining the power of Hoodoo dolls with candle magic. To bind the candle to the person, you can scratch their name into the wax. You can also carve a hole in the bottom of the candle and stuff it with taglocks, herbs, or other appropriate items and refill it with wax to seal it.

The most distinct type of Hoodoo doll is called a **poppet**. These are dolls that are made from scratch, with every element chosen to represent the person. These don't have to be complicated. Just take two pieces of fabric, colored appropriately depending on your goals, and cut out two human shapes, like a gingerbread man. Take those two pieces and sew them together, leaving a hole at the bottom where you can stuff your spiritual items. Sew the doll closed and customize it. Give the doll hair, clothes, birthmarks, an expression, or anything that further binds them to the person it's supposed to represent.

Using a Hoodoo Doll

If you can, make putting your Hoodoo doll together a part of the ritual by doing it at your altar. Simply building the Hoodoo doll isn't enough to give it power. You need to bring it to life. The first step is to tell the doll who it is. This is also called baptizing the doll: Sprinkle it with holy water and then say, "In the name of the Father, Son, and Holy Spirit who baptizes you as (person's name). Everything I do to this doll, I do to (person's name). Amen."

Now that your doll has been constructed, keep it in a safe place and interact with it daily based on your goals. For example, if you've made an effigy to increase your romantic and sexual attractiveness, you may want to kiss and caress the doll and keep it close to your bed. When you're not interacting with your doll, wrap it in a white cloth and store it away. Remember: everything you do to the doll, you do to the person.

When you feel your time with the doll is done, it's time to release

112

the spirit of the doll. Say these words over your doll: "Allow my words that connect you, set you free, so that you may return back to where you came. In the name of the Father, Son, and Holy Spirit. Amen."

Now that the spirit is released, you can dispose of your doll however you feel is right. You can disassemble it or give it a proper burial by burying it or throwing it into running water.

Hoodoo Doll Recipes

Just like mojo bags, these are incredibly personal, but it does help to have some sort of guide to how you should approach creating your own Hoodoo doll.

Love

- Base: Red or pink fabric

- Herbs: Rose petals, ginger, orris root, vanilla, peppermint

- Other: Carnelian stone, your taglock, the taglock of your beloved

If you want to make yourself attractive, construct one doll and customize it to look like you, focusing on all the things that make you attractive and lovable. If you'd like to attract a particular person, make one that resembles them with their taglock and join it with your doll with a cord.

Employment

- Base: Green or gold fabric

- Herbs: Nutmeg, Tonka bean, ginger, clove, cinnamon

- Other: Tourmaline, citrine, your taglock

While creating your doll, focus on your unique skills and all the things that make you a desirable employee.

Protection

- Base: White fabric

- Herbs: Copal, mandrake, juniper, frankincense

- Other: Onyx, quartz

As you construct your doll, light a candle and focus on the white light that encircles you. Visualize that white light as a force of protection.

Healing

- Base: White or blue fabric

- Herbs: Pine, ivy, carnation, rose, lemon balm, wintergreen

- Other: bloodstone

While customizing your doll, specify what you want to heal in as much detail as possible.

Conclusion

While we have an incredible amount of spiritual power, it's hard to manage our lives on our own. Mojo bags and Hoodoo dolls are invaluable allies that can help lighten our burden and act as a liaison between us and the spirits.

CHAPTER 6

Spells for Money, Luck, and Success

Now that you have all the pieces, it's time to start putting them together to complete more complicated and potent spells. The greater your knowledge of the tools of Hoodoo, the more you can customize your spells to meet your specific needs. Oftentimes, certain ingredients can be substituted for others as there is a lot of overlap in spiritual items, especially herbs. Just make sure to keep an eye out for signs of negative energy, mishandled spells, and spiritual attacks, so you can not only protect yourself from danger, but become the most powerful Hoodoo conjurer you can be.

To enhance these spells, set up your altar with a green or gold cloth and green candles. You can also include stones associated with prosperity such as peridot, pyrite, amethyst, citrine, or carnelian. You can also burn incense, burn the plant, or use the oils of the following herbs: Allspice, basil, buckeye, dill, mustard seed, or tonka bean.

Attract Money

This spell will help improve your luck in all things monetary.

You'll need: A red flannel bag, a garlic clove, sugar, whiskey, anvil dust or magnetic sand, a lodestone, a needle, and thread.

- Step One: Place the garlic and the lodestone in the bag.

- Step Two: Add the sugar and magnetic sand into the bag and sew it shut. As you sew, speak your monetary goals and needs over the bag.

- Step Three: Soak the bag in whiskey.

Money Candle Spell

This is also a spell for changing your monetary circumstances for the better. Your personal tastes and the types of magic rituals you prefer can help guide you choose how to approach your goals.

You'll need: A green candle, a sharp pin or needle, a bowl of water, and seven-star anise seeds.

- Step One: Engrave these words onto the candle: *Chrimata. Dirua. Maritupe.*

- Step Two: Light the green candle.

- Step Three: Toss the star anise seeds into the bowl of water one at a time. Each time you throw the seed, repeat these words, "*Sau ia ia te au chrimata. Sau ia ia te au dirua. Sau ia ia te au maritupe.* By the virtue of this seed, I will prosper. *Para chrimata. Para dirua. Para maritupe.* A little richer, I will be. Yes, I will, Yes I will be a little richer,*"* (Niare 2021).

- Step Four: Let the candle burn out completely.

- Step Five: Let the star anise seeds soak for seven days. After seven days, store the seeds in your wallet.

Win a Game

Perform this ritual whenever you want to secure a win at a competition or in gambling.

You'll need: An unused terracotta vase, a green silk ribbon, seven white candles, and seawater.

- Step One: Pour the water into the terracotta vase.

- Step Two: Place the candles in a circle around the vase and light them one by one while speaking these words, "O glorious Saint Lucia, who by the light has your name, hear me."

- Step Three: Wash the ribbon in the seawater while speaking these words three times (Niare 2021):

> I believe in God, the Almighty Father, the Creator of heaven and earth, and in Jesus Christ, his only Son, our Lord who was conceived of the Holy Spirit, was born of the Virgin Mary, suffered under Pontious Pilate, was crucified, died, and was buried. He descended into hell and on the third day he rose from the dead and he ascended to heaven. He sits at the right hand of God the Father Almighty. From there he will come to judge the living and the dead. I believe in the Holy Spirit, the Holy Catholic Church, the communion of saints, the remissions of sins, the resurrection of the flesh, eternal life. Amen. (p. 234)

- Step Four: Let the candles burn out.

- Step Five: Dry the ribbon out in the sun.

- Step Six: Carry the ribbon with you as a good luck amulet.

Moneyball

Use this spell to attract long-term prosperity. This spell will take a while to manifest so approach it with patience. This recipe uses Fast Cash oil, which, like many Hoodoo oils, can be homemade or purchased from local practitioners.

You'll need: Dry basil, High John the Conqueror Root, a green cotton thread, a piece of paper, and Fast Cash oil.

- Step One: Wrap the basil leaves around the High John root.

- Step Two: Write your name and your monetary goals on the piece of paper.

- Step Three: Wrap the paper around the basil and High John root with the thread 9 times. Leave a tail of thread so you can tie it up.

- Step Four: Coat the package with the Fast Cash oil.

- Step Five: Hang the package somewhere private.

- Step Six: Every day, make the package swing in a circle

and speak Psalm 23 over it. Feed it with money-related oil every week or so.

Debt Dissolved

If you're struggling with the burden of debt, use this spell to help you find a way out.

You'll need: Two medium red onions and a piece of paper.

- Step One: Write your name on the piece of paper nine times. Write the amount that you owe backward nine times.

- Step Two: Burn the piece of paper in your cauldron until it's complete ash.

- Step Three: Cut the onions in half and rub the ashes on the inside of each piece.

- Step Four: Place these onions in the corners of your home

Lucky Cologne

This cologne can be worn on your body to help you attract luck as you move through your life. However, you can also use it to add luck to any other spells or ritual tools to boost your rituals and make them more effective.

You'll need: Good quality rum, orange peels, and 9 nutmegs.

- Step One: Put the orange peels into the rum and let them sit.

- Step Two: As the orange peels steep, shake the bottle and speak these words over it, "This is a message to all my kin, above and below, please make me very lucky in wealth and in love," (Belard 2021). Repeat these words until you feel your wishes have been released into the bottle.

- Step Three: Set the bottle in the sunlight and let it sit. Repeat the prayer and shake the bottle once each day for nine days. The cologne is done on the ninth day.

Escape Poverty

If you're struggling on the brink of financial ruin, use this spell to find enough money to sustain yourself. This spell usually works best for modest amounts, such as $5000 or below. This spell isn't meant to give you a lavish life. Rather, it allows you to cover your basic needs.

You'll need: Ground ginger, black tea leaves, peppermint oil, a piece of paper, and a green seven-day candle.

- Step One: Poke three holes in the top of the candle and place a single drop of peppermint in one hole.

- Step Two: Mix the ginger and black tea and place the mixture in the other two holes.

- Step Three: On one side of the paper, write the amount of money you need. On the other side, write your name three times.

- Step Four: Burn the paper while speaking these words, "Holy ones, help me. Bring me a gift and grant me what I need," (Belard 2020). Repeat this phrase 12 times and blow out the candles.

- Step Five: Repeat this spell every day for seven days until the candle has burned out.

Lucky Bath Oil

This spell will help you attract luck in your daily life. If you make a large batch of this, you can keep it on hand and splash a bit into your bathwater anytime you feel you need a spiritual boost. You can have separate baths for hygiene and magic, or throw in a few drops every time you take a normal bath.

You'll need: Lavender essential oil, orange essential oil, olive oil, gold mica powder, and Citroen chips.

- Step One: Mix all the ingredients in a glass bottle.

- Step Two: Speak your intentions out loud, highlighting what area of life you want to find luck in as you put a few drops in the water. Meditate on these desires as you soak in the bath.

Get Lucky

If you feel like you've been struggling with a streak of bad luck, use this spell to help turn things around. This spell can help you deal with hard obstacles and ease your struggles.

You'll need: Incense ashes, parsley, a garlic clove, salt, and a silk white bag.

- Step One: Place the garlic, parsley, ashes, and salt into the bag.

- Step Two: Go to seven churches and dip the bag into the holy water font or stoup in each one. Each time you dip the bag, say the Lord's prayer, "Our Father, who art in Heaven, hallowed be thy name. Thy kingdom come. Thy will be done on Earth as it is in heaven. Give us this day our daily bread, lead us not into temptation and deliver us from our enemies who want us evil, and deliver me from my enemies who wish me evil. Amen," (Niare 2021).

- Step Three: Carry this bag around with you to cover yourself with good luck.

Big Man Cologne

This is a particularly masculine spell and will help you walk with confidence and healthy masculinity to help you achieve your goals. This cologne helps you become the type of person who succeeds.

You'll need: Lemon peel, lemongrass, juniper berries, dixie john root, bay leaves, and a cologne of your choosing.

- Step One: Put the herbs into the cologne.

- Step Two: Store the mixture in a cool, dark place for 12 days.

- Step Three: On the 12th day, shake the bottle and strain the herbs out of the mixture. Discard the herbs by burying them.

- Step Four: Rub the cologne on your wallet for monetary success. Rub it on your bed for romantic success. Rub it on your body to help find success in your day-to-day life.

Prosperity Wash

Everything you wash with this mixture will help imbue that thing with luck and help attract success in all things.

You'll need: A handful of peppermint leaves, a handful of magnolia petals, a handful of lemongrass, and 3 quarts of water.

- Step One: Place the herbs into the water and boil it. As it boils, speak Psalm 23 over the water.

- Step Two: Once the essence of the herbs has been infused into the water, strain the water into a bottle. Discard the spent herbs by placing them in running water.

- Step Three: Use the water to wash any place that you want to attract luck to once a week for five weeks.

Vase of Prosperity

This is a long-term ritual that will help attract luck to your household. This will affect not only you but all the inhabitants of the household and can help attract luck in household issues.

You'll need: A new terracotta jar, 7 rosemary leaves, 7 bay leaves, 7 basil leaves, 7 cloves, 7 lavender leaves, 7 thyme leaves, 3 gold candles, 3 green candles, 3 silver coins, a wooden stick, and oil.

- Step One: Place the herbs and coins into the terracotta jar and cover it with oil.

- Step Two: Place the candles in alternating colors around the jar in a circle and light them.

- Step Three: Stir the oil, herb, and coin mixture clockwise with the wooden stick while speaking these words seven times, "*Paisa. Panam. Pecunia. Penz. Para. Dirua*," (Niare 2021).

- Step Four: Stir the mixture counterclockwise while speaking these words seven times, "*Aurid. Arap. Znep. Manap. Asiap*," (Niare 2021).

- Step Five: Break the stick and drop it into the jar.

- Step Six: Let the candles burn out and keep the jar near a doorway or window.

Quick Cash

Use this spell when you have an urgent need for cash. This

simple spell is a quick and powerful way to get you out of a bind.

You'll need: Crushed bay leaves, powdered nutmeg, and powdered cinnamon.

- Step One: Mix the herbs and place them in a cauldron.

- Step Two: Light a candle and meditate on your specific monetary needs. Focus on why you need the money and the exact amount you need. Call out to the spirits and ask for what you need.

- Step Three: Burn the mixture and waft the smoke towards you so you can absorb the good luck.

- Step Four: Once the mixture fully burns, discard the ashes.

CHAPTER 7

Spells for Love and Friendship

It's not a surprise that love spells, also known as red magic, are so popular. Love is a universal and powerful emotion, and while everyone experiences it differently, everyone experiences it.

There's this belief that love potions cause some sort of madness in the affected person, that they force people into a zombie-like love stupor. However, that is not the case. Love spells create an environment conducive to forming romantic relationships. They create sparks and break down barriers that may be getting in the way of a relationship. Love spells can help a lot if you're struggling to connect with or flirt with the object of your affection, or if you feel they just don't notice you. They don't force emotions; they simply give emotions the environment to thrive.

Love spells are not without risk. There are black magic love spells that completely bypass a person's will that we will not be discussing due to the dangers for both conjurer and subject.

Love spells also can't fix problems of compatibility. If you aren't meant to be with someone, the spell and the spirits will try to communicate that with you. If you feel that something is wrong, it's best to stop the spell and reflect on the circumstances. It might be that the person doesn't have positive or genuine feelings for you. Many people have horror stories of performing love spells seeking the attention of someone who is already in a monogamous relationship. These stories never end well. It may also be that your feelings aren't as deep, genuine, or mature as you think they are.

Love spells aren't only used for romantic and sexual love. They can also be used to help with self-love, help you express your love to other people better, and enhance platonic and familial love. If you feel your life is devoid of love in any way, you can seek the help of a love spell. Love isn't a luxury. It's a human need.

Sweetening Jars

Sweetening jars are one of the most popular Hoodoo rituals due to their universality. Anyone can benefit from the effects of a sweetening jar, regardless of their circumstance. These rituals are used to 'sweeten' any aspect of a person's life, from a relationship, to self-love, to a job. They are also long-term spells. While the effects might take a while to be seen, sweetening jars can have profound effect over time. Sweetening jars require the following ingredients:

Jar

You'll need a glass jar with a metal lid for your sweetening jar spell. This is important because you'll be melting a candle on it, so you don't want the wax to melt any part of the jar. You also want the lid to have a tight fit so the wax doesn't drip inside the jar.

Sweetener

Sweetening jars are so called because one of their main ingredients is some sort of sweetening agent. The most common sweetener is honey, which is why many people refer to them as Honey jars. However, as long as it's a natural sweetener such as sugar, agave, or molasses, it will work.

Herbs

You can use any mixture of herbs according to your goals for your honey jar. You can always include herbs associated with love such as witch hazel, vanilla bean, saffron, and rosemary. As always, make sure to be purposeful about the herbs you include so that you aren't creating conflicting energies.

Petition Papers

Petition papers are a way to call out to the spirits and make specific requests. Historically, enslaved people used pieces of the brown paper bags their rations came in to write their petitions. You can also choose colored paper that reflects your goals.

Rip a three or so inch piece of paper with your fingers instead of cutting. Write the name of the person you want to target with your honey jar an odd number of times. Then, turn the paper and write your name the same number of times on top of their name. If the honey jar is meant to affect you, write your name on both sides. Once you've written the name, write a command without lifting the pen around the entire border of the paper. If you lift your pen, start the petition paper over again.

Taglocks and Charms

You'll need to include a taglock of both you and the person you're targeting. You can also include other spiritually significant items such as coins, magic charms, or stones.

How to Use a Honey Jar

- Step One: Put an appropriate holy oil or powder onto the petition paper.

- Step Two: Put your herbs and charms in the center of the paper and then start folding it. Fold the paper in half towards you, then turn the paper and fold it towards you again. Repeat this until you've made a packet. While you do this, speak your goals and intentions out loud.

- Step Three: Eat a dollop of your honey or other sweetener.

- Step Four: Add your sweetener, petition papers, herbs, taglocks, and charms into the jar.

- Step Five: Place your dressed candle on the top of the jar and let it burn all the way through. Repeat this every day for a week. After that, you can do it every three or four days a week. After a moment, burn a candle once a week or whenever you feel you need a boost to your spell.

- Step Six: When you've got what you desired from the jar, give it a proper burial.

Be Thought of Intensely

This spell will fill your beloved's mind with passionate thoughts about you and ensure you will not be forgotten or dismissed.

You'll need: A photograph of you, a photograph of your beloved, tape, a white candle, and a brand new mirror.

- Step One: Tape the picture of your beloved onto the mirror with their image facing the reflective surface.

- Step Two: Tape your picture to the back of the mirror with your image against the mirror's back.

- Step Three: Wrap the mirror and the pictures with tape.

- Step Four: Hold the mirror against your heart while speaking these words 49 times, "Every time you see your reflection you will think of me. *Thame. Skefteis*," (Niare 2021).

- Step Five: Let the candle burn out and put the mirror under your bed.

Attract Love, Luck, and Friends

This potion will help attract love in its purest form into your life. Whether you want to seek a new partner, meet new people, or simply make life a little bit brighter, this can do the trick.

You'll need: 3 strawberries, 3 tbsp. cocoa powder, 3 tbsp. salt, 3 vanilla pods, rose water, a saucepan, a piece of paper, a glass bottle, and a red marker.

- Step One: Pour the rose water, strawberries, cocoa, salt, and vanilla into the saucepan and boil on low for 30 minutes.

- Step Two: Write these words on a piece of paper with a red marker, "Pure love. Strong love. Open all the doors to me. Pure love. Strong friendship. Luck be favorable to me," (Niare 2021).

- Step Three: Put the piece of paper inside the glass bottle.

- Step Four: Strain the mixture and pour the liquid into the glass bottle over the piece of paper.

- Step Five: Shake the bottle and repeat the words you wrote on the paper seven times. Store the bottle in a cool, dark place.

Hair Love Spell

Getting the hair or other taglocks from a person may be difficult. You certainly don't want to do anything that violates a person's privacy or harms them. However, if you can get someone's hair, you can use it for powerful spells, especially in love. This spell is a basic but powerful spell to help someone fall for you.

You'll need: 5 strands of your beloved's hair, 5 strands of your hair, a red candle, a yellow candle, a green candle, and red wool thread.

- Step One: Place the candle in a triangle on the ground.

- Step Two: Tie your hair and your beloved's hair together with the red thread and place the bundle in between the candles.

- Step Three: Light the red candle, then the green candle, then the yellow candle in that order. Every time you light a candle, speak these words out loud: "*Ure, sanctus spiritus, renes nostros, et cor, nostrum, domine,*" (Niare 2021).

- Step Four: Let the candles burn out. Bury the bundle of hair near your beloved's home.

Make Them Fall in Love

This is a similar but more involved spell with a deeper intensity.

You'll need: Salt, a lock of your beloved's hair, nine yellow candles, nine green candles, and nine red candles.

- Step One: Make a circle of salt.

- Step Two: Place the candles along the salt circle in alternating colors.

- Step Three: Stand inside the circle and, starting with the candle facing east, light each candle one by one, moving clockwise.

- Step Four: Hold the lock of your beloved's hair, close your eyes and visualize them. Speak their name out loud 99 times.

- Step Five: Let the candles burn out. Put the lock of hair in your pillowcase.

Come My Way Orange

This charm will help create an atmosphere of love wherever it is planted.

You'll need: An orange, a rose petal, a lock of your hair, red thread, a needle, a small carving knife, nine pins, and Follow Me Boy oil.

- Step One: Anoint your hair, the needle, the thread, and the pins with the Follow Me Boy oil.

- Step Two: Roll your hair up into the rose petal.

- Step Three: Carve a hole in the orange and put the rose petal and hair into the hole.

- Step Four: Close the hole with the pins.

- Step Five: Weave the thread through the pins.

- Step Six: Bury the orange wherever you want an enhanced atmosphere of attraction, such as in a pot in your bedroom or by your phone.

Call Me Hand

If you've been performing spells intending to make yourself more attractive but haven't seen much change in your romantic life, it may be that your love interests simply haven't acted on their attraction to you. This spell will help you get contacted by a specific object of affection.

You'll need: A dime, a piece of paper, licorice root, and a purple cloth.

- Step One: Write the object of your affection's name on the piece of paper.

- Step Two: Wrap the paper around the dime and licorice root.

- Step Three: Wrap the package in the purple cloth while stating your goal out loud, "I want you to call me (person's name)."

- Step Four: Set the package on the floor and stomp on it nine times. Repeat this for the next nine days.

Ishtar's Love Ligament

This spell will help bind the Sumerian Goddess of love, Ishtar, to you and your life. This is especially good if you work with the Sumerian pantheon.

You'll need: One-meter long red silk ribbon.

- Step One: At night, tie a single knot in the ribbon while speaking these words out loud, "In the name of Ishtar, the one who makes everything fruitful, I tie you to me, and your love for me day by day as ivy on the wall will grow. So be it. So it will be."

- Step Two: Repeat this every night for 48 nights in a row.

- Step Three: At dawn on the 49th day, burn the ribbon at a crossroads and scatter the ashes.

Venus's Love Ligament

This is a similar spell that calls upon the Roman Goddess of love, Venus. You can modify these ligament spells to your own religious beliefs and magical practices to connect the spirits that control love to you and your love life.

You'll need: One of your hairs, one of your beloved's hairs, red thread, a needle, a wooden box, two pieces of paper, an apple, bay leaves, and a red candle.

- Step One: Prick your finger and write your name in blood on one piece of paper and the name of your beloved on the other.

- Step Two: Cut the apple in half and remove the seeds.

- Step Three: Tie your hair and your beloved's hair together.

- Step Four: Put the hair and the two pieces of paper in between the two halves of the apple and sew them back together.

- Step Five: Put the apple in the wooden box and cover it with bay leaves.

- Step Six: Close the box and light a red candle on top of it. As it burns, say these words out loud seven times, from Niare (2021):

> Venus mother, immortal Venus, daughter of Jupiter. To you who alone dominate nature and without you nothing is born. I invoke you and I

beg you. Let (person's name) quickly come to me. Make him fall madly in love with me. That he can no longer eat, drink, or sleep except with me. O Venus, glorious goddess, to you whom I said "If he does not love you already, he will do so soon" I address my humble beginning. Make him fall in love with me even against his will. So be it and so it will be. (p. 245)

- Step Seven: Let the candle burn out and keep it under your bed.

Love Me Mojo Bag

This mojo bag is constructed to enhance the love a specific person feels for you. This can be used to spark more passion in an existing romance or help push a 'more than friends' relationship into something more serious.

You'll need: A piece of paper, a pink or red pouch, a lodestone, hair from your beloved, and scrapings from the bottom of your beloved's shoe.

- Step One: Write your beloved's name on the piece of paper.

- Step Two: Put the piece of paper and all the other items

into the pouch.

- Step Three: Hold the bag to your heart and meditate on your intentions. Be clear, specific, and realistic about the type of love you wish to manifest.

- Step Four: Let the energy of your meditation absorb into the bag. Breathe on the bag and keep it close to your skin.

Think of Me

Use this spell to make sure you are always on your beloved's mind. This will boost the natural process of falling in love.

You'll need: 1 tbsp. thyme, 1 tbsp. crushed lodestone, a cup of your bathwater.

- Step One: Mix the thyme and lodestone in your bathwater.

- Step Two: Pour this mixture over the entryway of your beloved's door.

Bring a Lover Back

Use this ritual to bring a lost love back into your life.

You'll need: Red wine, a red candle, seven pieces of red paper, a black pen, scissors, and a glass jar.

- Step One: Cut seven hearts out of the paper and write these words on each heart: "(Person's name) cinta saya kembali kepada saya."

- Step Two: Light the red candle and say these words seven times, *"Keran scheva mencintai saya lagi. Kembalia kepada saya. Cinta saya lagi dan lagi"* (Niare 2021).

- Step Three: Pour the red wine into the jar.

- Step Four: Put a paper heart into the candle flame. Toss the burning heart into the red wine and say *"Kembali kepada saya"* (Niare 2021). Repeat this with all seven hearts.

- Step Five: Seal the jar and let the candle burn out. Store the jar under your bed.

Chapter 8

Spells for Protection and Spiritual Cleansing

Some of these spells are meant to protect your physical body, home, objects, etc. Protection spells are very popular for travelers or those who regularly enter dangerous or unknown territory. There are also several spells meant to protect your spiritual self. When we accept the existence of helpful and benevolent spirits and energies, we also accept the existence of harmful ones. Some of these spirits are called upon or come with negative emotions. Others are the result of people acting against us, whether unconsciously through wishing us ill or through direct magic curses. You cannot reach your peak as a conjurer if you do not take care of yourself. You have to protect and care for your mind, body, and soul so you can fully access your potential.

Cleansing Baths

If you're struggling with your spells and you're not getting the results you desire, it might be because you are carrying around negative energy and you need to purify yourself. Cleansing baths can be a helpful part of your regular routine as well to deal with acute negative energy. They can be used to reflect on the specifics of the ritual as well as your intention. For example, if you find yourself tied to someone who is negatively affecting your life, you can use cleansing baths to assist in severing those ties. You might also want to use a cleansing bath with a focus on protection before you embark on a journey or try a particularly difficult spell.

This cleansing bath ritual takes three days. You can consider it a deep cleanse that only needs to be done once a month. You can do smaller cleansing baths in between these deep cleanses whenever you feel you need one.

Day One

This day is meant to repel any negative spirits or energy that are connected to you. Do not do this ritual while menstruating as blood holds powerful magic that can disrupt cleansing.

You'll need: A few drops of ammonia, horehound, ½ cup of

vinegar, nettle, wormwood, yarrow, dandelion roots, red or purple flower petals, and two white candles.

- Step One: Just after sunset, run a bath of water as warm as is comfortable for you.

- Step Two: Set two candles on opposite ends of the bathtub to form a doorway that you will step through. Light them.

- Step Three: Add the herbs, ammonia, and vinegar. To avoid clogging up your drain, you can put the herbs in a tea bag or cheesecloth.

- Step Four: Step into the bath through the candles and fully immerse yourself. Meditate on the negative issues you want to be released and the positive things you want to attract.

- Step Five: Dunk your head under the water. When you come up, continue meditating on your desire to detach yourself from negative influences and achieve happiness and clarity. Repeat this at least seven times.

- Step Six: Get out of the bath through the doorway and allow yourself to air dry.

- Step Seven: Fill a cup with the bathwater and take it outside. Face west, hold up the cup and say these words:

"Whatever hold the negative forces or spirits have over me has been broken. I am free from every negative bond. As I cast this water over my head, I am also casting out every negative spirit and energy in my life."

- Step Eight: Toss the water out.

Day Two and Three

You'll be performing the same ritual for both days to ensure that you absorb all the positive energy that you desire. The second day starts the process, while the third locks it in place. You need to be clean for this ritual so take a regular bath or shower beforehand. Take this bath right before sunrise.

You'll need: An egg, milk, honey, cinnamon, nutmeg, comfrey leaves, allspice, hyssop, chamomile, angelica root, white flower petals, and two white candles.

- Step One: Run a warm bath and light the candles on the edge of the bathtub.

- Step Two: Crack the egg into the water, then add your herbs. Add the milk and honey last.

- Step Three: Step into the bathtub. Absorb the sweet smell, and let this guide your thoughts of all the positive things you want in the world.

147

- Step Four: Dunk your head into the water. Each time you come up, imagine yourself open to receive all the good things available to you. Repeat this at least five times.

- Step Five: Step out of the tub and let yourself air dry.

- Step Six: Fill a cup with the bathwater and take it outside. Face east, hold the cup above your head, and say these words, "I welcome this day with joy and gladness. I open myself to the blessing that the world has to offer me. I attract light, love, and positivity to every area of my life. I welcome all the good spirits into my heart and into my home."

- Step Seven: Toss the water towards the sun.

Prevent Harm

This is a very simple spell that you can use regularly to keep yourself covered by a veil of protection. All you need to do is go out to an open field at dawn and recite these words three times (Niare 2021):

> *Pater noster dei sanctorum. Maria bella angelorum.* Beautiful Mary sleeping. And the baby Jesus appeared to her in a dream. Dear, I dreamt that at the ordeal they brought

you. Golden crowns have lifted you up and thorns have planted you. What you are saying is truth, the Christ answered to your mother. And whoever says this three times in a field, is not afraid of water, thunder, and lightning. (p. 239)

Happiness Potion

Use this simple spell to help boost your overall joy in life. This potion can be applied to the skin and should be carried around as an amulet to attract and promote happiness. However, it is not safe to be ingested as pine needles can cause stomach irritation.

You'll need: An ampoule or vial, 1 dried and powdered dandelion, 1 tbsp. powdered thyme, 1 tbsp. powdered cinnamon, 1 tbsp. powdered oregano, and 7 pine needles.

- Step One: Place the herbs into the ampoule or vial.

- Step Two: Kneel facing east and, while holding the ampoule or vial in your hands, recite Psalm 7 out loud seven times.

- Step Three: Carry the ampoule or vial with you as an amulet.

Black Salt Powder

This powder is used to create a wall of protection around physical objects, such as your home, car, or expensive jewelry, although it can also be used to protect a person.

You'll need: Wood ash, salt, charcoal, and black pepper.

- Step One: Grind all the ingredients together in a clockwise motion until it is a fine powder.

- Step Two: Put the mixture into a bowl and speak Psalm 91 over it.

- Step Three: Surround anything you want to protect with a circle of the black salt.

Be Gone Fire

This spell is a way to burn away anything you want gone from your life. You'll need to have a clear and specific intention for this to work.

You'll need: White onion skin, lemongrass, peanut shells, bay leaves, and a fire pit or brazier.

- Step One: Light a fire in your fire pit or brazier.

- Step Two: Write the thing you want gone onto the bay leaf. If you want to get rid of multiple things, write each one on a different bay leaf.

- Step Three: Put the bay leaves, lemongrass, peanut shells, and onion skin into a bowl, and stir counterclockwise while speaking these words out loud, "That which I have written, send away forever" (Belard 2020).

- Step Four: Toss the mixture into the fire and don't inhale the smoke.

- Step Five: Once everything has been burned to ash and cooled, bury the ashes far away.

Hard Day Cleanse

If you've had a particularly difficult day or negative experience that has left you particularly weighed down, use this spell to restore your mind and soul.

You'll need: Eucalyptus leaves, lemon peels, rosemary leaves, peppermint leaves, and a cheesecloth.

- Step One: Tie the fresh herbs into the cheesecloth.

- Step Two: Run a hot bath and stir the bag in the water

counterclockwise, inhaling the aromatic stem as you do.

- Step Three: When the water is cool enough to be comfortable, fully submerge yourself in the water. As you come up, imagine yourself being filled with purifying light that will cleanse the negativity from you.

- Step Four: Get out of the bath and let yourself air dry. Bury the herbs far away.

Protect Me From Evil

Human beings have an incredible gift of intuition, and this is enhanced by the spiritual awareness that comes with being a Hoodoo practitioner. You will come to know when evil is around and affecting you. You'll be able to identify people who want to do you harm. This spell is meant to protect you or someone you care about from malicious intent.

You'll need: A piece of paper, cloves, dried onion, camphor essential oil, and a blue 7-day candle.

- Step One: Grind the clove and onion into a fine powder.

- Step Two: Poke three holes into the top of the candle.

- Step Three: Place four drops of the camphor oil into one hole.

- Step Four: Place some of the herb mixture into the other two holes.

- Step Five: Write your name or the name of the person you want to protect on the piece of paper and put it under the candle.

- Step Six: Light the candle and speak Psalm 91 over it while meditating on your goals.

- Step Seven: Let the first knob of the candle burn down. Repeat this ritual for seven days until the candle is burned out.

Save My Reputation

If you feel you're being unfairly targeted by lies and gossip, this spell can help you protect your good name and silence those who are trying to bring you down.

You'll need: Sunflower seeds, dirt from a crossroad, a piece of paper, a silver dime, string, and Stop gossip, Reversing, or Shut Up oil.

- Step One: Rip a piece of the paper off, leaving jagged edges, and write your name on it.

- Step Two: Put 9 drops of oil on the paper.

- Step Three: Put the dirt, dime, and sunflower seeds onto the paper and fold it. Secure the paper with the string.

- Step Four: Hold the package up to your lips and speak these words out loud, "I bind all that speak evil of me" (Belard 2020).

- Step Five: Carry the package on your person.

Find Serenity

If you find yourself plagued by uncertainty, anxiety, or emotional and spiritual chaos, use this spell to find your much needed peace. This spell should be performed under a full moon.

You'll need: 12 white candles.

- Step One: Make a circle with the white candles and stand inside.

- Step Two: As you light each candle one by one, speak these words: "*Sub tuum praesidium confugimus, sancta, Dei Genetrix, nostras deprecationes ne despicias in neccesitatibus, sed a periculis cunctis libera nos semper, Virgo gloriosa et benedicta. Amen*" (Niare 2021).

- Step Three: Meditate under the glow of the candlelight

and let negativity flow away from you.

Increase Your Power

Use this spell in times of weakness or when you feel drained and are struggling to live up to your true potential.

You'll need: Coconut milk, 2 tbsp. saffron, a white candle, and an unused sponge.

- Step One: Light the candle and speak these words without blinking, "*Aayan lese wura. Wura lese aayan.*"

- Step Two: Let the candle burn out.

- Step Three: Run a warm bath and add the coconut milk and saffron.

- Step Four: Soak in the water and wash with the sponge while repeating the words, "*Aayan lese wura. Wura lese aayan.*"

CHAPTER 9

Spells for Justice

As previously discussed, Hoodoo allows conjurers to use their abilities, with the assistance of the spirits, to harm those who deserve it. When you feel you've been put in an unfair situation or maliciously harmed, you can use Hoodoo to find justice on your own. While revenge might not fix a situation, it can bring peace and serve as a warning to others that would like to harm you.

Your ancestors will be especially willing to help you seek justice because many, if not all of them, lived without experiencing the justice they deserved. It's important to properly honor the ancestors you invoke through offerings, praise, and veneration. It's also important to pay attention to your state of mind and make sure your goal is actually *justice* and not solely *revenge*.

Anger is a powerful emotion and, if left unchecked, can bring great harm to the person experiencing it. However, with a clear head and a strong will, you don't have to fear seeking justice.

Stop the Evil Eye

Jealousy is truly dangerous. Those who covet what you have can cause you great spiritual harm, both intentionally and unintentionally. This spell will help protect you and free you from this harmful influence.

You'll need: A clove of garlic, oil, salt, water, a copper pot, three white candles, and a picture of the person who has cursed you with the evil eye.

- Step One: Place the candles in a circle around the copper pot. As you light each candle, speak these words out loud, "Glory to the Father and the Son and the Holy Spirit. As it was in the beginning, now and always, forever and ever, Amen."

- Step Two: Pour the water into the pot.

- Step Three: Rub the garlic onto the photo.

- Step Four: Chop up the garlic and toss it into the pot along with some of the salt and some of the oil.

- Step Five: Burn the photo in the flame of one of the candles and speak these words as it burns, "Garlic, sale, and oil. Go away evil eye; that I don't want you. Burn the evil eye. Broken is the enchantment. In the name of the Father, the Son, and the Holy Spirit" (Niare 2021).

- Step Six: Throw more of the salt and the oil into the pot.

- Step Seven: Let the candles burn out. Let the mixture sit overnight and, in the morning, toss it into running water white reciting three "Hail Marys" and three "Our Fathers."

Make It Stop

If you're facing legal proceedings and aren't prepared to deal with it, you can use this spell to slow things down and give you a chance to get ready. This won't stop the proceedings, but it will give you extra time.

You'll need: A jar, a piece of paper, and water.

- Step One: On the piece of paper, write down all the details of the court proceedings, including your worries.

- Step Two: Fill the jar with water. Put the paper inside and seal it.

- Step Three: Put the jar in the freezer. The spell will be active for as long as the jar stays frozen.

Protect Me From Harm

This spell is meant to protect you from abuse or injustice. It's particularly useful if you feel someone is after you or that they have tried and failed to cause you harm. This spell will help thwart all their attempts.

You'll need: Salt, oregano, liquor in a glass bottle, black feathers, and a piece of paper.

- Step One: Write the name of the person who is trying to harm you on the piece of paper.

- Step Two: Put the spices and feathers into the bottle of liquor. You can also say a protection prayer over the bottle as you do this.

- Step Three: Shake the bottle 11 times.

- Step Four: When you need protection, place it outside your back door. When you aren't using it, store it in a cool, dry place.

Hot Sauce Revenge

This is the magic equivalent of making someone wash their mouth with hot sauce. This spell will cause physical harm to your enemy. This harm won't be fatal or maiming, but it will be unpleasant. The hotter the sauce, the more intense the results.

You'll need: Hot sauce and a physical representation of the person (this can be a wax figure, a candle, a Hoodoo doll, etc.).

- Step One: Baptize the representation by telling it who it is. If you don't know the person's name, say, "Whoever did X to me."

- Step Two: Cover the representation completely in hot sauce.

- Step Three: Let representation sit in the sun. The spell will be active when the hot sauce dries.

Dry Up Their Love

This spell breaks romantic entanglements, not through a dramatic conflict, but by drying up the affection between them. You can use this to target a relationship started on false pretenses or born out of infidelity. You can also use this to lead someone to you.

You'll need: A rosebud, sand, salt, burned matches, two pieces of paper, a jar, and pins.

- Step One: Put equal parts sand and salt into a bowl and drop the burned matches inside.

- Step Two: On one piece of paper, write the name of your beloved. On the other side, write the person they are with.

- Step Three: Put the pieces of paper inside the rosebud and pierce it with the pins.

- Step Four: Pour the mixture of sand, salt and matches into the jar. Throw the rosebud inside and seal the jar.

- Step Five: Bury the jar in a graveyard.

Storm Head Work

This spell will rob your enemy of peace. It's important to make sure your intentions are specific and your mind is clear, or you risk setting that torment on yourself. For best results, do this spell right before a storm.

You'll need: A coconut, a black marker, black string, and water.

- Step One: Baptize the coconut by giving it the name of your enemy. Dip it into the water three times and repeat these words each time, "I baptize you (person's name). This coconut is now your head. Whatever happens to this coconut will happen to you."

- Step Two: Write what you want to happen to your enemy on the coconut.

- Step Three: Tie the coconut with string and hang it on a tree. When the storm is gone, check on the coconut. If it's gone, the spell has succeeded. If it's still there, activate it by breaking the coconut with a hammer.

Conclusion

You wouldn't know it from the mainstream media depictions of it, but Hoodoo is an endlessly beautiful practice. The spiritual realm is available to us in so many ways. Prayers, meditations, incense, oils, candles, herbs, and the gifts of the Earth, all grant us the power to be our best selves.

Hoodoo allows us, as black folks, to connect with our people. Disconnection from our ancestors has been a vicious weapon of our oppressors, an attempt to keep us from accessing our power, to make us feel weak and alone. Hoodoo represents bold defiance of this. It was born out of our ancestor's refusal to give in and let their culture and their spirits die. Hoodoo puts the power in our hands. It allows us as practitioners to be more than just pawns of fate. We can change the lives and circumstances of not only ourselves, but the people around us. No matter what you struggle with, you can start addressing it through Hoodoo.

I sincerely hope you've been inspired by this overview of the world of Hoodoo; I assure you that this is just the beginning. There is so much to discover about this practice that represents the work of generations upon generations. Whether you're using oils, candles, mojo bags, rootwork, or complex spell magic, I hope you approach conjuring with respect and intentionality. Respect the gifts the Earth has offered and the spiritual powers you have access to. Take care that the work you do comes from a thoughtful and honest desire to make things better, not only for yourself, but for your community as well.

Remember; as you take your first step of this journey, you are the culmination of all the dreams of our ancestors.

Thank You

"Happiness springs from doing good and helping others."
— Plato

Those who help others without any expectations in return experience more fulfillment, have higher levels of success, and live longer.

I want to create the opportunity for you to do this during this reading experience. For this, I have a very simple question... If it didn't cost you money, would you help someone you've never met before, even if you never got credit for it? If so, I want to ask for a favor on behalf of someone you do not know and likely never will. They are just like you and me, or perhaps how you were a few years ago...Less experienced, filled with the desire to help the world, seeking good information but not sure where to look...this is where you can help. The only way for us at Dreamlifepress to accomplish our mission of helping people on their spiritual growth journey is to first, reach them. And most people do judge a book by its reviews. So, if you have found this book helpful, would you please take a quick moment right now to leave an honest review of the book? It will cost you nothing and less than 60 seconds. Your review will help a stranger find this book and benefit from it.

One more person finds peace and happiness…one more person may find their passion in life…one more person experience a transformation that otherwise would never have happened…To make that come true, all you have to do is to leave a review. If you're on audible, click on the three dots in the top right of your screen, rate and review. If you're reading on a e-reader or kindle, just scroll to the bottom of the book, then swipe up and it will ask for a review. If this doesn't work, you can go to the book page on amazon or wherever store you purchased this from and leave a review from that page.

PS - If you feel good about helping an unknown person, you are my kind of people. I'm excited to continue helping you in your spiritual growth journey.

PPS - A little life hack - if you introduce something valuable to someone, they naturally associate that value to you. If you think this book can benefit anyone you know, send this book their way and build goodwill. From the bottom of my heart, thank you.

Your biggest fan – **Layla**

References

Belard, A. (2020). *Hoodoo for beginners: Working magic spells in rootwork and conjure with roots, herbs, candles, and oils.* Hentopan Publishing.

Hoffmaster, D. (2018, April 2). *Summer skin care tips and diy rosemary mint facial toner.* Suburbia Unwrapped. https://www.suburbia-unwrapped.com/summer-skin-care-made-easy-with-diy-rosemary-mint-facial-toner/

How to use your oils and candles. (n.d.). Hoodoo Hannah. Retrieved March 28, 2022, from https://www.hoodoohannah.com/how-to-use-your-oils

Niare, M., & Williamson, M. (2021). *Hoodoo: 4 books in 1 hoodoo for beginners + spell book + herbal magic + candle magic a complete guide to traditional folk magic.* Mamanu Niare.

Sasson, R. (2018, July 5). *How to do candle meditation and what are the benefits.* Success Consciousness. https://www.successconsciousness.com/blog/meditation/how-to-do-candle-meditation/

Siedlack, M. J. (2018). *Hoodoo (African spirituality beliefs and practices book 1)* (2nd ed.). Oshun Publications. (Original work published 2016)

Ward, K. (2021, March 9). *Your everything-you-need-to-know intro to candle magick.* Cosmopolitan. https://www.cosmopolitan.com/lifestyle/a31133533/candle-magic-colors-meaning/

Yumpu.com. (n.d.). *7 free magazines from hoodoo.conjure.com.* Yumpu.com. Retrieved March 28, 2022, from https://www.yumpu.com/user/hoodoo.conjure.com

Printed in Great Britain
by Amazon